Letters to

C000179108

(An Account of the Life of a British Army Staff Officer in Afghanistan)

By

Lyndon Robinson

To Will,

You would have thought your brother David would have got you something decent for christmas 2021. That said you will like page 313.

Yours age

Lyndon

Lt Col (Retd) L M Robinson

20th December 2021

Table of Contents

Dedication

This book is dedicated to the people of Afghanistan and to those with whom I served. It is also dedicated to the British Soldier who took the fight to the Taliban. I am less worthy than the least of those men and women.

Acknowledgements

This book was never my idea. All credit for this book goes to Alison Agnew, who had the idea to keep the village informed of my activities through regular postings on the parish website and who diligently captured each and every entry.

I would also like to thank Peter Doherty, a journalist who owned a successful media relations company. He spotted the potential of these website postings and identified that we could use these as a basis for a book. To this end, he labouriously proof read the entire tome.

Here, I should mention an important soul. During the publication of this book, Ryan Fernandez succumbed to Covid-19. He was a well-loved friend and colleague of all at Savvy Book Marketing to the extent that I feel he must be remembered by the self-publishing community in one of its books. So, here it is. Thank you, Ryan. May your soul rest in heaven.

Sarah Tye, Debbie Munford and Tim Dolder are also deserving of praise for maintaining my morale through their regular emails and for keeping me updated on village life while I was gone. I would also like to thank my old shipmate and crewman Phillip Poole, who, in his capacity as my Welsh reader, maintained my morale in the form of letters – that included some decidedly dodgy commentary.

I also feel that I should mention my old physical education teacher Geoff Lambrechts as he too cottoned on to the possibilities of this collection of missives.

I would also like to thank Sam Thomson, who, as a true schoolboy, had no love for writing letters, but he did manage to commit to correspondence on one occasion.

I want to give a huge collective thanks to the many villagers who celebrated my birthday in the Green Man, without me, I might add, and sent the video to me to prove it. Their many presents and endearing letters were a source of occasional unmanly moments; such was their generosity!

I must also thank Peter Geen, a gentleman with whom I am only marginally acquainted but who was, nevertheless, the first to send me a letter and the first to send me a Christmas card.

My reader in the Green Man is also deserving of a mention in this section.

The wonderful people that kept me sane were those with whom I was deployed, and I thanked them in person before leaving Theatre. They should really remain anonymous in order to avoid any embarrassment, but excusing rank and first names, Dorman, Hogendoorn, Howitz, Richter, Ulloth, Van Keulen and Zandee were quite remarkable. Indeed, Ulloth is probably one of the finest sergeant majors of any Army in the world.

Finally, I wish to acknowledge the support of my wife, our two daughters and the rest of my family, who committed me to the care of Afghanistan.

20th January 2012

About the Author

Lieutenant Colonel Lyndon Robinson was born and raised in Buckinghamshire in 1961. He was educated locally, having been placed in a permanent foster home when he was four years old. He grew up with seven foster brothers and sisters, who consider him their own flesh and blood.

He read Fishery Science at Plymouth Polytechnic, during which he also worked as a fisherman on trawlers out of Brixham. After a brief spell as a management trainee with McDonald's, he was commissioned into the Royal Corps of Transport. He specialised in amphibious operations and consequently commanded his own ship, Her Majesty's Army Vessel Ardennes. As his career matured, he developed into a general logistician and served in Northern Ireland, the Balkans, Iraq and Afghanistan. While in Afghanistan, he was involved in developing the capabilities of the Afghan National Army and the Afghan National Police.

The author also happens to be a former rugby player of no real achievement. His interests include amateur dramatics, campanology and poetry. Success has eluded him in all these pursuits, but he was once delighted to discover one of his poems languishing in a library in Northern Ireland.

He has consistently failed to learn French but ploughs on regardless. He and his wife Eleanor have two daughters, and they live in a rural community. Lieutenant Colonel Lyndon Robinson wrote on the Mursley village website using the nom de guerre Garry Lee-Sumvill. He is a Christian.

Letters to a Village is a collection of the author's writings on the Mursley village website, sorted in chronological order from June 2011 to January 2012.

Foreword

This is a story of how a comfortable village in Middle England came face to face with the Taliban.

Mursley in Buckinghamshire could be described, with some accuracy, as an affluent rural idyll. Its 600 plus inhabitants have been largely unscathed by the recession, and its picturesque main street is dotted with thatched cottages and gleaming four-wheel drives. It has a vibrant village life that revolves around a pub, a church and a little junior school.

The Afghan war was something one watched on Newsnight – a troublesome affair in another world, a long way from home.

It also seemed a world away from Lyndon Robinson. About to turn 50, the father-of-two teenage girls wasn't your typical squaddie. For most of his friends and neighbours, both his rank and his soldiering were something of an enigma.

True, the regimental flag flying daily from a mast in his garden left no doubts about his endearingly eccentric passion for the military. But he was better known for his bell-ringing, amateur dramatics – or lending his efforts to erecting marquees at the church fete.

Then Lieutenant Colonel Lyndon Robinson received the call, and everything changed. Plucked by the Ministry from the green fields and leafy lanes of the Home Counties, he was planted 4,500 miles away in the midst of the chaos, confusion and catastrophe that is the war-torn Kabul.

His new home was a cramped container in a military compound, subject to occasional danger and shared by soldiers of every creed, colour and culture that make up a multi-national force.

It may have lacked modern comfort or convenience, but it offered access to the Internet. And thanks to technology, a little won spare time, and a previously undiscovered talent for what can only be described as exceptional journalism, something remarkable emerged.

The Colonel's daily, candid yet endearingly cheerful and constructive observations of life on operations were posted on the Mursley website and became mandatory reading for many people in his village.

For six months, thanks to the writings of Lyndon Robinson, a whole village stood face to face with the Taliban – and gained a unique insight into the gritty reality of life for many of those involved in the biggest cultural conflict of the early 21st century.

- **Peter Doherty**

Introduction

While the subject matter is grave, this is not a serious tome. It is simply a collection of jottings that seek to capture the life of a British Army Staff Officer in Afghanistan during Britain's fourth Afghan War. The book reflects the interpretations of the author only, many of which are highly subjective. For the student of International Affairs, it holds little. It holds even less for those who have an interest in the study of war. For the serious-minded, it may well be a disappointment.

What it does give, though, is a series of asides by an officer sent to Afghanistan to do a job against a backdrop of defence restructuring – and what that might mean personally. The work, therefore, may be of value to those whose interests lie more in social sciences; the poems especially so. The aim of this book is twofold: Keeping the reader amused while developing in him or her a deep respect for our soldiers who operate in their name.

The account carefully avoids identifying the work undertaken and those involved as this would detract from the theme and may present security challenges. However, the inquisitive reader could draw out from these jottings seven aspects of interest against which one could measure further research. They can be summarised as the '7Cs':

- ☐ Command
- ☐ Control
- ☐ Capability
- ☐ Commitment
- ☐ Cash
- ☐ Culture
- ☐ Corruption

These yardsticks would also need to be used in the Afghan and ISAF context against political, social, historical and military criteria. If you understand the 7Cs and their relationship to one another, you will understand this campaign.

All that is, however, for the academics. This is an undemanding study written with a patron of the Green Man public house in mind. It should therefore be read with a beer.

June 2011: Atkin's Rant

What plea can a dead soldier make,
For his mates adrift in the Afghan take?
Green benches are polished by England's greed,
And blood is fertile for the Afghan weed.

Why, as a nation, do the best of breed fight,
And lesser men take votes and a mistress at night?
These fumbling bumbling self-righteous take alls,
Care not for Tommies in mortared mess halls.

What plea can a dead soldier make,
To those grown fat on England's take?
More troops to share the working-class burden,
And damn your greed, you fatted vermin.

27th June 2011: A Glass of Water and a Biscuit

Well, not quite a cable from Kabul as I'm still on route. We left at 0240 on a Monday morning. I moved left after boarding the aircraft to what I think folk would describe as Economy Plus. Our young soldiers (God bless them) moved to the right. Later I had a bit of a conscience and went aft to see how they were. The plane was not full, and being economy, they were able to raise the armrests and had created cots for themselves. Meanwhile, their officers were trying to configure their bodies into the slightly wider Economy Plus seats. The lads think there is some justice in the world.

On dozing off in our chartered airline, I was woken to be given a glass of water and a biscuit. I then dozed off again only to think it would be more comfortable were I to take my boots off. Big mistake as the pilot then announced we were landing in Germany. This we did. We were ordered off the plane as it was refuelling and sent to what passes for a departure lounge. It did have some luxuries, including a widescreen TV. This was showing a shopping channel where young women were modelling brassieres. I thought this was a little inappropriate, what with over a hundred blokes about to become intimately acquainted with celibacy. Still, there would have been a riot if I'd complained.

In the Middle East, we waited for a C17 aircraft, which is better designed for a Theatre of operations. We will then board and move on. If you ever want to know what soldiers are thinking, read the graffiti in the toilets. One example was in French, which I was able to translate. It was none too complimentary about the British out here.

29th June 2011: Ruthlessly Professional

Having changed planes, we moved on to a main operating base in Afghanistan. The hull of a C17 aircraft has a couple of portaloos and about four portholes. As is normal on landing, we were invited to fasten our seat belts and, unlike commercial air travel, don our body armour and helmets. The air steward, who was a big burly Sergeant, said the lights would be dimmed. They were. . . it was pitch black bar some red glows somewhere in the inky black void.

The landing was like any other, only it was night time and still very hot. Confused, tired and disorientated, we were subjected to briefings and then lugged our weapons, rucks and grips to a coach, which was nicely decorated by its driver with frilly curtains, lace and such like. I'm coming to the view that the Army pays us for what they put us through rather than what we do.

We started early the following morning and had a shed load more briefings. Everything was covered, from Afghan culture to offensive operations. I had some personal offensive operations dealing with a disturbed digestive system, but perhaps I should not go there. Food is OK, but the climate is hot to hotter; even the cutlery melts!

That was our first day. Today we were subjected to more training, which included a few hours on the ranges firing our weapons while wearing helmets, body armour and anything else that was heavy. Normally I have trouble hitting a cow's backside with a spade at three paces. Today I surprised myself and did some of the finest shooting of my career.

This may, in part, be because I'd been given an assault rifle with a bipod and optical sights. The accompanying bayonet did have me pondering, mind. I wasn't bad with the pistol either, albeit I did ask to shoot again.

During our environmental health brief, we were warned about all the nasties, including rodents. We were told not to do what some soldiers had done, which was to capture a rat and cover it with the luminous fluid from a Cyalume (a chemical light). The now green orb would then dart about the place, causing some amusement.

This was rightly deemed unacceptable, and matters then turned to snakes, scorpions, sand flies. . .

I know my comments are somewhat light-hearted, and I intend to continue in that fashion in order to amuse. What is not light-hearted is the actuality of what we are doing here.

This is ruthlessly professional and would make for a difficult read.

July 2011: My Mate Jack Daniels

At five or six, I was tied to a gate,
With a packet of crisps on a plastic plate.
The firemen that came and cut me free,
Responded to the cries of help from me.

Well, social services they had a view,
And I no longer lived at Twenty-Two.
They found me a home by the sea,
Where the air was warm and the beatings free.

Now a kid in care, at some new school,
The bullies who bruised had one rule.
Quick with my fists, I learned to prosper,
But it profited me, not a home no longer.

Out on my ear, rejected twice,
The Army appealed. It looked nice.
And my mum's lover said it did him no harm,
The pay was good for an early alarm.

And they sent me to - Iraq and Stan,
Where I shot and killed many a man.
Bandaged a kid minus his face,
My mate Jack Daniels died in the place.

But it was all meant to be,
And life in the Army suited me.
Up I went from one to two,
Stripes on the Arm in the recce platoon.

Proud was I, I'd done well for myself,
But around the corner was death by stealth.
It came when they sacked me an unwilling Redundee,
Before I'd turned nigh Twenty-Three.

Rejected now thrice I returned to my Mum,
But she'd set up home with another bum.
He threw me out for his own two sprogs,
I was on the streets with the rats and the dogs.

Now a geezer up the road called Razor Steve,
Had a job for one who could hurt with ease.
But I couldn't do it; to hurt folk bad,

It was against the values the Army had.

But Razor he laughed and scoffed did he,
What values were those bequeathed to me?
I'd swallowed it whole, or so he said,
For Generals' sleep in a pensioned bed.

I turned down the job for what it's worth,
I considered myself of nobler birth.
But now, as a sit below a tree,
The memories come back and damage me.

On the TV, it said the Army's a recruitin',
The boys no longer the Taliban a shootin'.
But I've lost my job, and my mind's shot through.
I have a new friend; he's called Jack too.

1st July: Like Chickens

I have been at this main operating base for four days now. However, in order to get to my destination, I have now been called forward for my final in Theatre air move. There have been yet more briefings and an episode in what is called a roldem. In effect, this is a full-size model of an armoured fighting vehicle which is bolted front and back to two large wheels, one at each end. The truck is in effect the axis. There was some delay to our being herded into this contraption so that a young Royal Marine could clear up his sick.

Once the eight of us were inside, the instructor then rolled it to 90 degrees, and we had to then effect an escape having been harnessed in. When doing this for real, the harness is necessary to stop you flying about inside in the event of an Improvised Explosive Device (IED), as well as keeping you in place should the vehicle roll.

We mastered the 90 degrees, so the operator then rolled it 180 degrees, and we repeated the exercise. The temperature inside was 45 degrees. We were in helmets, body armour, and the like, suspended upside down like chickens in a slaughterhouse. Dust, muck and darkness... it's how I recollect it. No wonder the young commando had earlier parted with his lunch. Good training mind, but I was wondering about my career choice at this juncture.

Small, Medium and Liar

In briefings, we were told to wear our tier one and tier two protection when on patrol. Tier one is like a pair of heavy Lycra cycling shorts, and tier two the external codpiece. These must be worn – and to emphasise the point, we were shown two graphic photographs of soldiers who had been IED'd. The one who was wearing this kit could have children; the other could not. We felt for the lads regardless. Humour has it that the codpiece comes in three sizes, small, medium and liar.

Cultural Awareness

We were given more cultural awareness training and told that breaking wind was utterly unacceptable to the Afghans. A shame, really, as the occasional well-timed love puff is a source of much amusement to the British soldier.

We were also told that we might be asked about our religion. Responding that you are an atheist is a no-no. They find this abhorrent, as they cannot understand where you would get your moral compass from. Instead, the Afghan cultural advisor said to us that if we were asked and were atheists, we should tell them that we were Christians or Jews. Our soldiers appeared to have no problem with this. Well, it's certainly no problem for me as a Christian.

Well, I must sign off, as I'll be moving on shortly. Not sure when I will be able to make my next post. Also, I've to go and wake a young soldier. He asked me to do so in order not to miss the flight. How the Army has changed! Maybe I should make him a cup of tea.

2nd July 2011: Not a Tourist

I signed off my last missive to say that I might make a soldier a cup of tea before I woke him for his flight. Well, I did. He must be the only soldier in the British Army not to drink tea!

It was hot to hotter when we flew out, which reminded me of advice about sunbathing. Soldiers were only allowed to do so in PT kit, having also applied sun cream and been made aware of the need to hydrate. The Garrison Sergeant Major caught one lad sunbathing with nothing more than a sock entombing his credentials. The lad may have been given a rifting, but the laughter sure boosted morale.

I am now at my destination, having spent the night in a tent with some eight strangers.

To get there, I had moved through the city in an armoured convoy. While doing so, the lad riding top cover asked me to go up and join him. The view through my protective goggles left me scrambling for adjectives. I do not know how to describe it. The bustle, the dust, the decay. The smog. Four people on a single motorbike. Children waving. Pedestrians crossing almost oblivious to the traffic. Carts piled high being pulled by a single elderly bloke. Vehicles being serviced on the road. No sign of any health and safety.

Cables, wires, potholes and a sea of people in organised confusion. Houses, donkeys, a city and mountains all in the same view. Mudbrick walls, walls with holes. Exhaust fumes, horns, no traffic regulations, checkpoints, AK47 armed police. A myriad of observations flooded the senses.

I could have forgotten that the lad next to me was constantly scanning his environment for danger, as in fact was I. I had to pinch myself that I was a soldier and not a tourist.

3rd July 2011: Nothing Like Making an Impression

A good start to my tour, I thought, as I strolled into breakfast. There are so many nationalities here it resembles the bar scene from Star Wars. Having got my grub (more of that later), I sought out a seat.

I spotted a table of several French soldiers, which I thought was an excellent opportunity to practise my French. How was I to know they were a very senior French General and his staff? Still, there is nothing like making an impression, I say.

Plethora of Firearms

The good lord, in his wisdom, placed my "cell" near to the chapel. This is good as the Sunday morning service starts at 0830. My only friend here thus far is Jesus but there, as part of the small choir (four in number), was a Major who had served on my ship. It was great to see him, although his singing hasn't improved.

The service was American in style with plenty of modern hymns. Some of which were so modern I suspect neither Bey Christian nor Margaret Dowding back in the village would know them. I certainly didn't. A lot of Brits were present, which was nice, but the plethora of firearms wasn't.

Tiresome Things, Bullets

I have now met my "cell" mate. He was not the huge Mongolian I had feared but a small intelligence officer from the United States who loves his family. He's been here for over a year and told me in four days he will be gone. Oh no, I thought, a huge Mongolian is bound to be his replacement. It's a modern world, and I have been told that if you have any worries, make it clear that there is no kissing on a first date and that a first date lasts six months!

Returning to the subject of food, I am very mindful that for our lads out on the forward operating bases, the offering here would be a banquet from heaven, so I should just be grateful and shut up. However, it would not pass muster in a British Army cookhouse, although British livestock of the porcine variety would love it.

Must go now and account for my ammunition—tiresome things, bullets, especially when I appear to have been given so many of them. I do hope the Sergeant Major doesn't want them all back.

4th July 2011: Inspirational Service

It's 4th July here, and the Americans were making a song and dance of it. I mean that literally as I joined in an Independence Day service. They called it an "inspirational service", which I assumed meant it would be of the Pentecostal tradition. Well, whatever tradition it was, it was African American centric. They were leaping all over the place, which put a staid Anglican like me in a bit of a position. I did, however, tap my foot to the beat of the drums, organ and trio on vocals. I thought about inviting them over to Mursley Church, but I don't think we are ready for it!

Struggling With the Language

I am getting some clarity as to what it is they want me to do here. As I do not speak American, I am struggling a bit with the language. It's either that, or I fully understand what they mean, and my subconscious is rejecting the message!

Prayers Welcome

I seem to have been adopted by the Dutch quarter. The base is made up of cantons from different nations. They have decorated their areas with symbols characteristic of their homeland. The Dutch have a windmill and the Canadians ice hockey regalia. We Brits seem to have settled on a huge Union flag, which appeared to be unduly prominent today.

As the Dutch speak perfect English, I have no problem, and they serve the best coffee on the camp.

The news regarding one of our soldiers today was upsetting, but then it always is. I understand it has reached the British media. What appears not to is how other nations are suffering too. Prayers are welcome here.

5th July 2011: Some of Them Should Be

The Union flag, which during yesterday's Independence Day I had found somewhat amusing, was today flying at half-mast. Prayers are now really simple. Please, God, let it not be half-mast again.

I have written in the past about the need for soldiers out here to remain hydrated. By way of an aid, I noticed in the loo a colour chart showing shades from dark, meaning dehydrated, to almost transparent, meaning hydrated. Presumably, one gazes at one's pee, observes the colour, and then checks it against the appropriate colour code.

This I did and can report that of the several shades to choose from, I was "optimum". Well, that was a relief. However, I did form the view that such was the mess that some folk may have felt, it was like a pregnancy test, and you had to actually aim at the chart.

There was also another notice asking patrons not to flush tampons down the toilet. This rather amused me as I was definitely in the men's and such a product is not the usual accoutrement of the British male. Maybe foreign men are different, after all.

We do live cheek by jowl, and there isn't a lot of privacy. Morning showers are like something out of a state pen. I have decided that European males are not fussed about nudity, and to be honest, some of them should be. We are told to shower for no more than three minutes, which is one minute longer than when I was attached to the Royal Navy.

The Frozen Chosen

My cellmate who is off home tomorrow is a southern Baptist. He describes his faith as the "frozen chosen", such is their lack of demonstrative behaviour in church. That tickled me until later when he was trying to comfort a young son who was upset at his dad being away so long. Clearly, the excitement of his Pa coming home was too much for the boy.

Earlier I'd spoken to a US Sergeant starting a 12-month tour with a two-year-old daughter who she will not see for at least six months. Her husband, she told me, was looking after their girl. As he was US Special Ops, I had an image of some SAS type trying to change a nappy, which amused me.

If the Taliban Don't Get You, the Toryban Just Might

There has been much talk among us out here about redundancy. It seems some are trying to remain in Theatre in order to avoid being made redundant. Lose your life or your livelihood. If the Taliban don't get you, the Toryban could. That's perhaps a little political, so I'll sign off now.

6th July 2011: Jesus Was Never Lost

I finished my last report on the subject of redundancy. My Christian friend, the Major whom I have already written about, has submitted his application for voluntary redundancy. He told me that five years ago, he'd found Jesus and that he and his wife would use the money to fund their planned missionary work in Africa.

The funny thing was, the preacher told him that he hadn't found Jesus as Jesus was never lost! This has been a long journey for Adrian as I remember only too clearly over a decade ago his coming to church with me in the Isle of Man only to go again to a different denomination later in the day. Strikes me he's been searching for a while.

Pink and Runny

We sat down for dinner last night, and yes, there was a wow factor as we were served huge T-bone steaks. My American friend cut into his and announced that it was pink and runny, just how he liked it. He then threw it away for fear of food poisoning. "Chomper" here had no such qualms. After my mother's cooking, I have a stomach like asbestos (well, almost. . . see earlier jottings).

Tourniquets Already in Place

Earlier conversation proved less attractive. The subject to hand was personal security. We've been told that when deploying outside the Green Zone, one must do so having prepared for contact. This means helmet, body armour, rifle, pistol, ammunition, morphine, ballistic glasses, ID discs, tier-one underpants and a tourniquet.

The trouble is if you are going to a ministry building resembling Rambo, it may not help the customs issue you are trying to resolve. But then again, if there is a contact, a lightly slung pistol is hardly an act of war. The fear is a Mumbai style encounter where the insurgents go from room to room shooting people.

Who do you engage? They may be dressed as police? In the heat of the moment, how can you tell? The logical thing to do is to wait for them to shoot at you. You will then have positively identified your enemy. However, at this juncture, they may well have terminated any intent on your part.

On the subject of tourniquets, they are an individual issue designed to allow the soldier to apply them to the stump of his arm or leg. The Sergeant who had briefed us on their use, demonstrated how to do so and urged us to practise on ourselves.

You cannot necessarily expect your mate to do so because if you have been IED'd, then you are in effect in a minefield. Your mates will need to clear a safe passage. This will take time during which you could "bleed out". One soldier we are told was "lucky" in that the explosion cauterised his stumps and stopped the bleeding. Word has it that some American soldiers fear the worst and patrol with tourniquets already in place. We need a new word for courage out here to be applied to the infantry whose annual earnings wouldn't amount to a politician's expenses.

My roommate has now gone home. He didn't so much as get up but rather floated out of bed. He left me a two Euro coin and his Harley Davidson calendar. I wonder what my new roommate will be like. . .

8th July 2011: Absolute Crap

As I gazed through my mosquito net this morning at the wire encrusted rubble fortification that serves as a back garden, I thought to myself... this is absolute crap! The five and half hours' sleep did nothing for my thumping headache.

As I crunched on aspirin and quinine washed down with warm water, I remonstrated with myself for being so ungrateful. I reminded myself that it was far worse for our teenagers fighting and dying in the forward operating bases (FOBs). That said, they were at least surrounded by their mates who love them, whereas I was effectively in a sea of strangers made up of the ambitious, the homesick and those dodging redundancy!

A Gender-Reassignment Process

Yesterday as we ruminated over our dinner, the Dutchman expressed surprise at the prominent ponytail worn by a German Lieutenant Colonel. A conversation rapidly ensued as to regulations governing hair length in European armies. Somebody more knowledgeable as to the circumstances piped up. There was a general consensus that this must be the absolute last place in the world where you would want to be undergoing a gender reassignment process.

The German Lieutenant Colonel who was in the process of doing so commanded our absolute respect and admiration.

Feathers Flying

I was amused the other day by an American giving a description as to how he saw staff work: *"I want you to pluck the chicken. I do not care how you do it just pluck it. If I don't see feathers flying I just know the chicken isn't getting plucked."*

That said, he didn't use the word "pluck".

More Luxurious Setup

My new cellmate arrived last night. He'd flown in from a main operating base (MOB) and is a Commander in the Royal Navy. He complained that it was 51 degrees at the MOB when he went through what I'd gone through.

He appeared somewhat knackered. Having tried to make our cell nice, he nevertheless announced that he would be moving out at the first opportunity as the fellow from whom he was taking over had a far more luxurious set up which included an armchair. Well, there's gratitude for you. I'm now more than convinced I'm going to end up with a Mongolian.

Parting Shot

As a parting shot (excuse the pun), I would just like to report that in the mornings, I'm getting an urge to vomit. Folk, tell me it might be altitude sickness as we are 6000 feet up here. I hope it doesn't last.

By the way, the German Lieutenant Colonel to whom I referred to earlier does by all accounts live in my block. This presumably gives an indication as to which way the process is going.

I bumped into a German doctor this morning and did what the medical profession hates, namely mentioning an ailment outside of surgery. This ailment being my morning sickness. Much to my relief, he told me I wasn't pregnant and that I was most likely having an adverse reaction to the altitude.

From what he said, I am certainly fairing much better than most. He also counselled that on returning to the UK, I should do my annual fitness assessments as my red blood cells will have increased so aiding performance.

Working Long Hours

I have to report that I am working long hours. Yesterday I finished at 2300, and today I got away early at 2200. With a start at 0730, after a gym session at 0600, I am not sure I can keep the pace. Tomorrow I've to facilitate a brief to a lot of important people about an issue that is facing the Theatre.

I have never had to concentrate so intensely while feeling so rough in at least 15 years. If the brief goes well, then the General may well keep me in Theatre. If it goes badly, then he may be looking to lose me and send me home. Either way, redundancy is a real prospect early next year. Therefore, from a resettlement perspective, I'm being incentivised to make a right Horlicks of said event, so that I can get home and better prepare for civilian life.

I'll let you know how I get on, and if you see me walking down Mursley Main Street next week, don't ask.

Go for the Main Body

The team of which I am a part had cause to travel on foot to another fortification in the Garrison area. Once outside the main gate, we were accosted by small children begging and trying to sell trinkets. You had to harden your heart and just press on. I'm sure many readers will have experienced similar things when on holiday in the third world.

The children were obviously a distraction, and I fell behind the main body. I was, however, accompanied by a pureblood Navaho Indian and on seeing this situation unfold, I suggested that we catch up. I was told that this was not wise. Should a suicide bomber just happen to be passing, he would obviously go for the main body and ignore us. Not a lot, one can say, really.

Poetry and Piss

Due to the volume of work I'm currently doing, I began to wonder this afternoon if I was being dumped on from a great height. I needn't have wondered because I was. A sharp stench of urine assaulted my nasal cavity while I was bashing away on my keyboard.

A sewage pipe outside the office door that ran down the side of an adjacent building experienced what an engineer would describe as a "catastrophic failure". This caused a rush of water to explode majestically into a shower of noxious pong that twinkled star-like in the golden rays of a beating sun. Poetry and piss. What more can I say?

9th July 2011: A Cool Stare

Regular readers of this column will be aware of the importance of today's conference, and that failure on my part would perhaps mean a one-way ticket home followed by the displeasure of an American General.

As the great and the good mustered to see my downfall, all was in control. The seating plan was done, and the video telephone conference purred into life. *"Hello xxxx this is xxxx, over,"* says I in my best Army Officer accent. A sinking depressing mental aroma of failure assaulted my senses when I realised that I couldn't hear the outstations, which meant nor would the Generals.

Yes, I know I should have done my technical checks earlier, but I couldn't for reasons aplenty. As I mentally packed my rucksack for the flight home, one of the many Generals called the meeting to order. A cool stare wafted across the table, and the thirty folks in the room followed his eyeballs as they settled on an emotionally destitute Brit. We were off. Relying heavily on skills acquired treading the boards with the Mursley Players, I opened my brief. Two hours later and the meeting closed—no flight bookings. The boy survived to fight another day.

Flip Flop Encased Tootsies

Having had a crap day prompts me to comment on the toilet doors. They are so close to the pan that when you close them, having nestled your buttocks onto the porcelain, your feet stick boldly out into the abutting passageway.

On the other side of said passageway sits a row of basins. The obvious advantage of this is that you can tell immediately which toilet is free in the event that the local food demands some fast action. The disadvantage is when some 300lb German, reversing from one of the basins, settles on your flip flop encased tootsies.

Afghan Lollipop Lady

This location doesn't just include Germans but many different nationalities. All with different uniforms, some of which it has to be said are in the Elton John style. While military fashion is perhaps a third-order issue, the paying of compliments, i.e. saluting, isn't. To simplify things, High Command has instructed that only officers of the status of Brigadier or above are to be saluted. Such is the myriad of different rank slides; this ruling isn't as helpful as it might first appear. I'm convinced that this morning I saluted an Afghan lollipop lady.

Jar of Yak Fat

My cellmate has yet to move out. This is just as well as a Mongolian soldier carrying an AK47 smiling at me in the chow line. An Afghan veteran friend of mine assures me I should only start worrying if he has a jar of yak fat. As it happens, he didn't.

10th July 2011: Was Popular in His Village

The young NCO sat earnestly listening to the brief given by the intelligence officer. He had to; it might just save his life. The lad wasn't long in Theatre, and the Taliban were already changing their tactics.

"Listen up: suicide bombers are no longer young. The old are deemed expendable and are being encouraged to do the right thing for a Taliban pension pot. They are going to die anyway so why not earn their loved ones a few quid in the process."

It was hot that day. The sun beat remorselessly, and the sweat steamed the ballistic goggles held firmly against his face. As the snake patrol formation weaved its way, his thoughts turned to home.

An elderly bloke hoved into view, walking purposefully towards his patrol. The NCO had been trained; he knew the drill. So did the Afghans. When approaching a patrol: stop. Lift your clothing and show that you are not wearing a suicide vest.

But this bloke wasn't stopping. The patrol looked anxiously at their leader, fear sweeping across their faces.

35

The NCO's pulse quickened, and the words of the Int officer coursed through his brain, searing his mind at the implication of what might happen.

He shouted a warning. The Afghan kept coming. He shouted again and then a warning shot. But the Afghan still kept coming. Thoughts of home were now exploding in his mind as he desperately wrestled with the inevitability of his training. Please, please stop. His patrol, their faces now tortured with fear, screamed at him to do something, just bloody do something.

The Afghan fell dead. A single well-aimed shot from a trembling fire position ended his life.

The elderly man was popular in his village. He just loved to go out and greet every patrol that passed his way. It was the highlight of his day. But medical care was never up to much, and he being deaf and partially sighted was always a worry to those who loved him.

11th July 2011: The Chaplain Is Trained in Such Matters

The flag flying at half-mast was what greeted me as I made my way to a breakfast of what resembled wallpaper glue and two slices of French toast. Another lad lost in the cauldron that is Afghanistan who would have been only too happy to eat with me today.

Regular readers of my jottings will be aware of my complaints about the possibility of my being made redundant when I return to the UK. My woes, however, are nothing as compared with others. My Dutch friend has asked for redundancy but has been denied. It appears that the Dutch government is negotiating a reduction in their severance package, but the military trade union is resisting. I never thought I'd be sympathetic to the idea of a union in a military organisation.

A senior colleague confided in me that before he deployed, his wife was declared clear from cancer. . . but she isn't now. My advice was fairly abrupt. There are a hundred thousand of us out here, and he will not be missed. Well, he will be by me as he is a thoroughly nice bloke. Another chap has been sent out here to do a job for which he has been specially trained.

The trouble is the task is too large, and he is suffering from mental exhaustion. I've been there and, as a consequence, was removed from the post, which while very damaging to my career, did mean I kept my health and good looks. Well, maybe not the looks! He does not want to fail, as it will cost him his promotion, so he is driving himself to a nervous breakdown. I told him to go to church. The Chaplain is trained in such matters.

He Hopes to Disappoint Her

I'd noticed a soldier always eating alone in the cookhouse. I thought that this can't be right and decided to ruin his day by leaving my colleagues and joining him. He was from a tribe of very special air soldiers and was working long hours. In his downtime, he was attending to legal correspondence.

He is separated from his wife, who is demanding custody on the grounds that he is an unsuitable father because he is suffering from post-traumatic stress disorder. As a consequence, he has to see a psychiatrist, which he feels is a complete waste of his time as he is fine. Indeed, unlike my earlier friend, he did appear to be OK.

Moreover, his wife will not divorce him. The nature of his work means there is a likelihood of death and were that to happen, she would not get the death in service payout. This is a large sum of money paid to widows of those who die in service. He hopes to disappoint her by not getting killed.

12th July 2011: Eat More of It

As I glanced at the breakfast offerings, which included olives, I was minded to question the menu choice when something more outlandish caught my eye. There were posters in the cookhouse, encouraging us to eat more healthily.

A traffic light system had been developed where the offerings were colour coded. Food which was labelled green was good for you and you should eat more of it. That which was labelled brown suggested you should help yourself to moderate portions whilst that which was labelled red you should eat less of. Well, I'm no killjoy in the cookhouse, but I felt that this initiative, whilst laudable, had certain presentational and practical challenges. Firstly, our lads are fighting for their lives out in the FOBs, and I'm sure it will be a comfort for them to know that their High Command is worried about what it eats.

It's not that I'm criticising. It's just that we must be careful not to become remote from the sharp end. Secondly, and this is where a vested interest kicks in, I noticed that one of the food groups labelled green was cabbage.

Now we share rooms here. Imagine the shock of seeing your roommate consume vast quantities of cabbage over dinner. You just know you are in for a night of aromatic acoustics. No. . . they should definitely think these things through.

Home on Compassionate

A colleague of whom I have already mentioned went home today on compassionate. I'm glad he did so. He loves his wife, and as I said to him, there are a hundred thousand of us out here, and he will not be missed. The last part was a lie. He will be missed. He was a superb officer and is a huge loss to me. My job will be far tougher and more unpleasant for his going.

13th July 2011: Religious Literature Abounds

I've decided that our Rector, Laurence Meering, would like it out here. Well, no, not really, but he would like the faith aspects. It is unusual being in a community where Christianity trumps secularism at every turn. Obviously, there are lots of very religious Americans but also Catholics from Poland and other Eastern European countries.

Religious literature abounds, and the other day I returned to my desk to find prayer cards by my keyboard. Clearly, some kind soul felt I needed them! The polish General has a crucifix of Jesus on his wall in an obvious position by his desk. However, the waist-high wooden crosses mounted on stands by every desk have no religious purpose. They carry your body armour and helmet.

It's nice to be in the majority for a change rather than that swathe of secularism that we get at home. Indeed, I have learnt never to immediately engage an American in conversation if he sits down next to you with his meal. The first thing he or she will do is say a silent prayer. Mind you, sometimes looking at the grub, I'm minded to do so as well.

Feeling the need for spiritual inspiration, I went along to the evening service populated by my African American friends. The singing was just fantastic, and I could just imagine Bey Christian and Margaret Dowding getting stuck in with the best of them. There I was, enjoying the worship when it came to the sign of peace. Now, as you know, in our church, it consists of a handshake. You may also get a kiss on the cheek and a light hug if the going is good. I'm not normally that demonstrative, but hey ho, I go with the flow.

This was an altogether different experience. I tried to slip out the back, but it was too late. Never before in my life have I been hugged by Mike Tyson lookalikes in the uniform of the United States Marines. Things got a bit heavy after that, and a pulped and squeezed British friend of yours was only too pleased to return to his seat.

The preacher opened up with a fiery sermon and exhorted the soldiers not to commit adultery. A fat chance of that, I thought, surrounded as I was by ebony muscle. What a lovely bunch of folks they were. . . Christianity in all its joy. Maybe next week I'll pick up with the C of E folk. Sadly, however, their service is scheduled during the working day and extricating myself maybe a bit of a challenge. Hence why I joined my fellow Americans.

Before closing and without getting too emotional and sloppy, I can tell you for a fact that were I not an imperfect Christian, I could not cope with it out here.

14th July 2011: Srebrenica

My recent missive describing the joy of sharing a church service with predominantly African American soldiers brings little comfort today. Our French colleagues have suffered enormously, and the French Special Forces lads with whom I had dinner this evening were decidedly downtrodden. I extended my sympathies in my best French, and while they were very appreciative, I did at least raise a smile as I struggled with my French grammar.

Maybe recent experiences have informed other conversations. One Dutch soldier described his experiences in Srebrenica in 1995 when the Serbs massacred thousands of Muslims who had sought sanctuary with the Dutch Battalion. He explained that the Dutch soldiers were low on ammunition and short of supplies and that close air support was denied to them.

As the Serb Divisions closed in on them, their CO was told by Ratco Mladic that the Dutch could either go or accept the consequences. The CO decided to take his soldiers out. The soldier telling this story said that subsequently, he suffered mental health problems but that he was over it now.

For two of his comrades, however, there was no recovery. The sense of shame proved too much, and they killed themselves. Two Dutch lads have asked me to review their CVs in English after there was much talk of being made redundant. One of them was at Srebrenica.

15th July 2011: Semper Fi

As I bimbled back to my cell at 2300 after a busy day, I encountered a 6'4" shaven-headed American having a difficult time in the ablutions. He was complaining of feeling faint with gut ache compounded by the fact that he couldn't get any movement aft.

He said that despite wanting to, he just could not rid himself of the source of his discomfort. Well, I could hardly leave the poor fellow, could I, so I encouraged him to one more last effort. Semper Fi (Always Faithful: the motto of the USMC) and all that.

I'm sure the floor trembled as my eardrums were assaulted by what sounded like a fire hydrant peppered with air bubbles. I was expecting some explosions here in Afghanistan, but nothing like this. The groan of relief was audible, so I said cheerio and left him to the follow-up action.

As I then made my way to my scratcher (Army slang for bed), I pitied his cellmate being mindful that for me, that particular trap (toilet) was no longer an option. Apparently, there is a bug going about. A bug? More like an elephant.

Married His Mother in Law

A chap over breakfast told us a story about how a group of Afghans with whom he was travelling were teasing one of their numbers remorselessly. The poor bloke was recently made a widower, which frankly wasn't anything to laugh about at all.

It appears that since the loss of his wife, he had married his mother-in-law, which was the source of the Afghans' amusement. I'm saying nothing.

16th July 2011: Joined a Slimming Club

This morning I met my American colleague who was in such a two and eight the other night in the ablutions. He told me he was fine now, but he did look decidedly slimmer. I apologise if my description was somewhat graphic, but I thought my reader in the Green Man would want to feel as close as possible to my experiences. Well, perhaps not that close.

I've joined a slimming club. Well, I haven't, really. It's just that the weight does appear to be falling away. Since being in Theatre, I have lost 5Ibs. There are perhaps several reasons for this. The heat acting as an appetite suppressant being one. The food also acting as an appetite suppressant, being the second. But the greatest contributor is perhaps the long working days.

Mournful Bunch

Unlike when I was in Iraq, I haven't seen a single rat. A Frenchman, yes, but no rats. This may be because of all the wild cats that festoon themselves around the place.

We are under strict orders not to feed them. They do appear to have far longer canines than our domestic moggies and are excellent tree climbers. They do not bother me, mind and if they remove the rats, then who is arguing. The dogs outside the compound are a sorry looking lot, and I discovered a female Lieutenant Colonel buying a tin of ham to feed them. With rabies being prevalent, I have not got too close, but they do look a mournful bunch, and I can sympathise with dog lovers wanting to help them.

Different From the Dutch

I'm still chomping on my anti-malaria tablets, having been ordered to do so. I take two a day and a double dose every Monday. We must be different from the Dutch because their doctors tell them they do not need to take them. I did have a young British soldier express concern because he didn't have any, so I gave him some of mine. After he tasted them, I am not sure that he was grateful.

They Just Take Bribes

We Brits here are the victims of raised eyebrows and smart comments. It seems the unfolding Media scandal has rather trashed the British reputation for honesty and integrity. We are now no longer in any moral position to complain to the Afghans about their corruption. They just take bribes. It's us that intrude on private grief and employ those that do. There's more honesty, decency and integrity in the back of a British Army mastiff than among that lot. It's especially shameful considering what our teenagers are doing out here. Now that I've got that off my chest, I'm going to find out what that meowing is.

17th July 2011: What Is Scotland?

You will not be surprised to hear that I have met a few Afghans. A statement of the blindingly obvious, I suppose, seeing as how I am in their country. A couple were rather surprised when I sat down next to them and introduced myself. I suppose they were not accustomed to a British Army officer being so approachable.

As the conversation developed, I couldn't get a word in edgeways, which, as you know, is somewhat unusual for me. They were on permanent send and expressed a keen interest in Britain and our religion. I tried to explain that the United Kingdom wasn't just England but also consisted of Scotland, Wales and Northern Ireland.

I had to laugh when they asked me what Scotland was. It's only my fondness for Campbell Thomson that prevented me from milking that particular line of questioning. They could speak several languages, and fortunately, one such language was English! They were obviously highly intelligent. I have to confess to feeling somewhat humbled, especially when I realised that these lads were cleaners. Well, actually one was a school-teacher who cleaned in order to top up his salary.

They were both worried about the security situation and getting slotted when travelling to and from work. Imagine living in fear like that? Such fear has another Afghan, who is our interpreter, desperately trying to get a visa to America. He had served with our ground forces and, for his trouble, was shot twice. The pity of it all is that this country needs bright young men like him, but one cannot really blame him for wanting to make a new life for himself. Getting shot once is enough for any man, but twice!

Man Love Thursday

There is, however, a side to the Afghan culture that gets an occasional mention and, to be honest, appears all rather strange to me. There is a phrase here called "Man love Thursday".

At one outpost, we were cautioned that on Thursdays, we shouldn't move around the base alone after dark. With a face like a dropped pie, I have to confess I didn't feel threatened. It was later pointed out to me that while that may be so, I was, however, clean-shaven. Strap back. I'm a portly geezer with a face like a bulldog licking a thistle, closer to 50 than 49, and somebody is seriously suggesting that I'm a good catch for an Afghan male who takes a day off from his sexuality on a Thursday.

I suppose I should be flattered.

18th July 2011: Greater Men Than You

I am coming to believe that life in Afghanistan is one of the extremes. At one end, there is the utter heartbreaking and gut-wrenching awareness of the sheer awfulness of what our soldiers are going through.

Daily I see the incident reports, which describe in clear, concise military language what has happened on the ground. You learn that one of our lads is hurt, you pray for his recovery and then later the news comes in. . . "DOW". Died of Wounds.

Meanwhile, the Union flag is once again being run up and then back down to half-mast. You try not to think about the lad's mates and those who love him for fear of being distracted from your duties. Later, you walk back to the block. Your sense of manhood cheapened by the knowledge that there are far greater men than you, half your age, carrying the burden of a nation.

He Looked Like One

Then comes the complete and the absolutely absurd. Take this morning, for example. There I was, walking back from the showers, when I was distracted by a male form in female underwear. I was speechless until I realised it was our German colleague on whom I have already commented. Then later we learn of the Block Manager who fields complaints about the accommodation.

By all accounts, an American phoned him to protest that while he was shaving, a chap on the adjacent basin was doing likewise. Nothing wrong with that I hear you say only the bloke was shaving his testicles. The American continued to report that it was an Italian and when asked how he knew, stated he looked like one!

19th July 2011: Thirty-Seven-Digit Experience

The British taxpayer, in the act of benevolence, provides a soldier with thirty minutes of free calls home a week.

To access this service, you have to find a "paradigm" phone and then dial the paradigm number, followed by your user number and then your password. This requires you to dial in 26 digits and then the telephone number.

Overall this is a 37-digit experience. Sadly 30 minutes is adequate. When one of our lads is killed, the service is cut to ensure that his or her next of kin is notified through the proper channels. This seems to happen a lot, and when I cannot ring home, I am reminded of the grief that a family will be going through.

It Doesn't Happen in Uniform

I met a contractor. He works three months on and one month off with door-to-door club class flights home. All paid for by the taxpayer. I do not begrudge him a penny. After all, he is a former infantry soldier who fought at Fallujah, Iraq. It's good to see the lads dip in. It doesn't happen in uniform!

Constipated Yodeller

You may recall the Naval Commander who moved out of my cell on the pretext of a better offer, namely a cell with an armchair in it. He approached me yesterday, having had a rough night's sleep and asked if he could come back.

His new cellmate is an Albanian who snores like a constipated yodeller. I'm sure I can lose the Full Bird Colonel who has moved in with me. He, too, was complaining. His complaint was being tired due to having been woken up by machine-gun fire, which I am guessing was when an advisor to President Karzai was killed. Old Rip-Van here heard nothing. Me? I can sleep on a washing line in a Force 10 gale.

20th July 2011: Fingers in Your Ears

The good news is that I will not be selected for redundancy in the autumn. The bad news is that such matters have been moved to early next year. All my efforts at redundancy dodging have therefore proved utterly fruitless. I'm beginning to feel that somebody is having a laugh at my expense.

I have now finished helping my Dutch colleague with his CV and covering letter. Hopefully, he can now concentrate fully on the matter at hand, namely a war. Talking of which, we had a recent flap when somebody thought they had discovered a bomb.

The announcement was made over the tannoy in what I thought was Macedonian. As it happens, it was in perfect English, but the speaker quality is suspect, and it is hard to hear when you are hiding under your desk with your fingers in your ears.

Medieval Codpiece

What is it about folks that no matter what they buy or wear, it has to be fashionable? Take, for example, the wearing of firearms. I have a 1980s temperate pattern camouflaged holster with canvas trim.

It was all the QM had. It does, however, clash somewhat alarmingly with my desert pattern uniform, but being of rustic stock, this is of no consequence to me. For others, however, this would be a no-no. We have a range of colours, designs and body positioning that is daily paraded as these military fashionistas walk to breakfast.

There are some holsters made of moulded plastic, which jut manfully from the leg that are resplendent of a medieval codpiece. Others have elasticised lanyards. Some dangle down to the knee whilst others are held tight on the belt.

I am, however, not a complete fashion embarrassment and did fall prey to a rather natty chest holster worn on my body armour. This should give me a rather Ramboesque appearance, but sadly, for me, the ensemble is more Rumpole than Rambo.

21st July 2011: High Ranking Underpants

We have a contract laundry on post and have accordingly been issued a white net bag with a number on it. The drill is that you put your washing in the bag and then sign it over to the laundry. We have even been instructed as to how to fill the bag by use of a diagram.

The entire bag is shoved into the machine, so if you overfill it, the wash will be of poor quality, and if you underfill it, then you are wasting resources. There is another reason for not overfilling your bag, although this is not specified. You have to plan on losing it, so never allow yourself to sustain such a loss as to render yourself pantiless. I got that tip when I was in Iraq.

On queuing to sign over my bag, I noticed the Admiral in front of me. The routine is essentially blunt and grunt. *"Initials?"* and in my case, *"LR"* comes the reply. However, with the Admiral, the laundry attendant scrawled across his chit "VIP" in big, bold capital letters. How does one have "VIP" laundry? Is the laundry bag treated with greater reverence than your average soldier's skiddies?

Are the high-ranking underpants saluted as they are ceremoniously placed in the tumble dryer? It's all a mystery to me, but it is good to see that rank still has its privileges. The Indian lad who signs over the laundry does this day in and day out. He never smiles, so I thanked him in his mother tongue. He gave me a huge broad grin revealing a set of perfect white gnashers. He didn't, however, write "VIP" across my laundry chit.

22nd July 2011: The Attention Span of a Politician's IQ

My lone reader in the Green Man will know that unlike most folks, I frequently encounter a superior mind. I discovered yesterday that working with the Afghans is no exception to this rule.

We had a long meeting which was exploring the opening staff work attendant with solving a very challenging Theatre problem. Being military, we have a process for thinking. I know this will come as a surprise to my pinko liberal friends, but we do.

In the US Army, it is called the military decision-making process, and in ours, it may be described as the combat estimate. Put simply, when the military is given a problem, it applies this process in order to work out how to resolve said difficulty. Without going into the details, you have to clearly understand what the problem is, know your constraints, assumptions and tasks and then identify several courses of action (options), each of which you test against established criteria.

It is not strictly a linear process. It allows for both the art and science of war, and when it is finished, you then have a course of action and can move into the order's process. This is what my liberal friends don't like, namely telling people what they are required to achieve and underpinning it with military discipline. There are, however, perhaps three necessary skills to this methodology.

Firstly, you have got to understand it; secondly, the process must be quick enough so that you break the enemy's OODA Loop (Observe, Orientate, Decide, and Act) and finally, on occasions, you have to be robust enough to think straight whilst physically exhausted and potentially in peril. Now I know all this because once upon a time I did a course on it!

In broad terms, it involves seven steps, and yesterday we waded through the first one. It was complex and briefed in American using the PowerPoint medium. We were talking some fifty detailed slides. I was beginning to resemble a cross-eyed mongoose with the attention span of a politician's IQ when our Afghan colleague piped up with one question which he had formulated from the mass of detail in front of him.

In poor English, he succinctly summed up his point. And what a point it was. Over to you General to field that one. Third world army with first world brains. . . respect.

23 July 2011: Pythonesque in Its Satirical Brilliance

Reports from the media that the Government is to lose one in five of Her Majesty's soldiers by 2020 has gone down like a lead balloon. Almost Pythonesque, in its satirical brilliance, it has folks here gulping for expletives.

Your country needs you . . . well maybe not.

I know that such little matters shouldn't be allowed to get to you but out here, keeping a lid on impotent rage is hard work. For an army to be successful, its High Command must have a moral courage that is commensurate with the physical courage of its soldiers.

I'm sure all is in hand. Nobody, however, wants to see retired Generals dozing on the red benches of Westminster Palace while redundant soldiers sleep fitfully on the park benches of Westminster Gardens.

A 19-year-old soldier spoke to me about the redundancies. I told him he shouldn't worry; it's the old farts like me that will be thinned out. He smiled at the thought of me being an old fart.

My smile, however, was somewhat more forced. He's stuck out here in the middle of Afghanistan. Could I really tell him what I actually thought? One in five is double decimation. Mapping a career round that will be a challenge. In this conversation, did I lack the moral courage that seconds ago I wrote so earnestly about?

Flip-flop Endowed Taliban

Today, of all things, I was invited to a VIP lunch. I knew it was a VIP lunch because the room where it was being held had "VIP" written on the door. My last VIP experience was, as you know, the laundry chit episode.

As it happens, I saw the Admiral in church but decided not to ask after his underpants. It would have been entirely inappropriate as this was, after all, a typical Anglican service; there were eight of us! Not that that in any way diminished what was a superb communion, and I was grateful to the Padre for trekking down to see us.

Returning to my theme of the VIP lunch, it was in honour of a visiting General who wanted to sound out opinions on pre-deployment training and events in Afghanistan. Well, you know exactly where this was going. I'm a gabbler me, and one swig of root beer had me singing like a canary. Well, after yesterday's news, they could hardly sack me twice, could they?

I made the not inconsequential point that our grandparents' generation won the First World War in four years. Our parents' generation won the Second World War in five years, and yet our generation was, after ten years, still trying to subdue the flip-flop endowed Taliban with some 49 countries arraigned against them, including the all-powerful Americans.

I then made some observations as to why this should be despite the incredible bravery of our soldiers (God bless them). Fearing a violent shove out the door and an urgent missive to the senior British Commander, I was pleasantly surprised to note that my comments were warmly received. The point of my frustration is that, as you know from the media, the politicians want us to withdraw combat troops by 2014 and that such a withdrawal should be conditions-based. Well, guess who is part of a team running around with their hair on fire trying to sort out in 12 months one of those conditions?

As an aside, and to add to my woes, I am assuming that my old mucker Colin Kempthorn is continuing his run of success in the Friday night Green Man-meat raffle? Please don't answer that it will only upset me.

24 July 2011: Nibbles to the Nether Regions

The local insect life seems to be dining out á la Robinson. I'm waking up in the morning with several bites about my person. Fortunately, my combat underpants being of a tight fit ensure that there are no nibbles to the nether regions. Still, circumstances are causing a degree of discomfort, so I have taken to bathing myself with insect repellent prior to entering my scratcher. I now know where the term "scratcher" comes from.

Mixed Views

Having finished her tour a colleague left for Blighty the other day. She mentioned that she had mixed views about going home. On the one hand, she was simply over the moon, but on the other hand, she hated leaving her team behind and would fret accordingly. This is the problem with sending folks on operations as individuals. It is far better to deploy as a formed body and go home as a formed body. There are no residual worries as you know your people are safe.

English Is the Language of Choice

The team of which I am a part is some 20 in number consisting of ten different nationalities. English is the language of choice, although I am sure I have picked up some Czech expletives.

Because for many of us, English is a second language, you have to listen intently to what is being said. Our Afghans have to understand English delivered by those for whom it is not their first language. Now, this must be extremely difficult, but to their credit, the Afghans appear to manage. There is, of course, the potential for some amusement and my Dutch colleague's pronunciation of "fakir" did make me smile.

The possibility of embarrassment also exists, and a British Colonel had to prompt a senior American female officer not to use a particular phrase. This phrase would have been completely misunderstood by a Brit, and I suspect, would leave him feeling rather hopeful.

25 July 2011: Nobody Important

I thought my reader in the Green Man would like to know about my average working week, and when I say week, I mean week. I say average because occasionally I have to go off and do things. In essence, reveille is at 0550 when I rise from my scratcher and bimble bleary-eyed to the block ablutions. We have our own form of the "Dawn Chorus" out here and to be perfectly frank, there is nothing worse than masses of males in the throes of bulk abluting. The only sense not to be molested is taste, or at least I think it is.

By 06:10, I am in the gym for my 30-minute workout. The grunting established earlier in the morning seems to continue as our American cousins stack the bar with weight and then exhale loudly with the exertion of it all. Meanwhile, yours truly in his union jack tee shirt is embarrassing himself wrestling with a dumbbell favoured by the Jane Fonda workout crowd.

By 07:00, I have showered and am in the breakfast queue listening to anything from Queen to country and western. To be honest, breakfast isn't bad, providing you stick with what you know. The bacon and eggs are an absolute horror, but again the Americans seem to love it.

72

At 07:30, I am listening to the morning's stand up brief, which describes events over the last 24 hours. Obviously, all cannot be at the actual presentation, so we attend virtually and have to enter our names and log in accordingly. As people do so, their names ping up on a list adjacent to the PowerPoint slide that is being briefed at the time. Some virtual attendees are obviously quite grand. There are Generals, Brigadiers, Colonels and all sorts.

There is the rank in abundance. Wondering who all these people were, I did on one occasion scroll down the list only to find somebody had entered his details as "nobody important". I saw this as a brave attempt to burst the bubble of military pomposity, but it seemed strangely out of context considering the sheer awfulness of what was being described.

At about noon, I break for an hour's lunch and do so again at 18:00 for dinner. If I finish by 20:30, I'm pleased. This, however, is rare because not only have I a job to do, but I also have to learn about the Theatre's wider perspective in order to improve my situational awareness. The pace of work is not steady. It's the staff officer's equivalent of circuit training.

On Friday, I am lucky, as ISAF doesn't start work until 13:00. However, because I'm a Brit, I am unlucky as there are UK centric briefings that require my attendance. There is also a late start on Sunday when kick-off is at 10:00. Clearly, what I have described is not the same for everybody. The base is on the go 24/7, with shift workers constantly at work. When I go to the gym, many folks are already up and about. The following morning the cycle repeats itself with me and "nobody important" listening in on the misery of the previous 24 hours.

26 July 2011: Oooh Er Missus

In my last update, I mentioned the term situational awareness, which in plain English is knowing what is going on. I must have tempted fate as the boss suggested that he should improve his situational awareness by doing a battlefield circulation.

This is not a British Army term, but I wasn't slow in picking up what it meant. When it was discussed, I was considering what pre-briefs the boss would want when all of a sudden, I was in the frame to go with him. What me? Oooh er, missus!

As the late great Frankie Howerd would say, "Frankly (excuse the pun), it will be fine". Important people like my boss get shed loads of protection, and guess who'll be hiding amongst it! My main worry is being sick on the helicopter. Those pilots don't 'alf throw them about.

Ogle

Now I'm not really a conversation stopper, but I was a little irritated the other day. Some officers (not British, I might add) were commenting on the attributes of a female soldier. One of them leaned over and inquired as to my thoughts. I told them I had far too much respect for the

75

British soldier as to ogle one of their number. That brought the conversation to an abrupt halt, and they looked a bit sheepish for having embarrassed themselves.

We German's Don't Need Invitations

There are, without doubt, cultural differences amongst us soldiers out here. The Dutch were planning a meal, and while making conversation, I asked the German if he'd been invited. *"We Germans don't need invitations,"* he replied.

Now we were in Fawlty Towers territory, and I was more than happy to go there. I think he took it well when I told him they'd invited themselves to England in 1940, but we'd refused them entry. Well, he did laugh, which is just as well as I'd overlooked the fact that he was a six-foot-tall German paratrooper.

Yak Fat, Anyone?

It's official. My cellmate is moving out. As he is senior to me, he is entitled to a better class of cell. My matelot colleague has let me down as he has found alternative accommodation. The Albanian snorer had proved too much, and the Commander couldn't wait for a wink longer. Yak fat, anyone?

The Mercy of the Coalition

Somebody, please spare me the indignities. There I am, late in the evening, trying to make sense of a report written with about as much clarity as a sweep's spectacles when my dog and bone rings.

It's the Commanding Officer phoning to say that he will phone again on the 1st September to let me know whether I have been made redundant or not, rather that I will not have been, because I am on operations. It is not as if he didn't realise the farce of it all because he did, but the Ministry required this conversation to have taken place.

I then suggested that notwithstanding the war, could he possibly have a word, as I really didn't mind being given the order of the boot. Unlike the bloke phoning me, I hadn't volunteered for redundancy, so I remain at the mercy of the Coalition Government. Meanwhile, on the radio, the rock band Europe is playing . . . the final countdown.

But there's more. The day of indignities goes on. Keeping hydrated as ordered, one has to frequent the loo. There I am in the throes of pointing Percy at the porcelain as an Afghan squats down using his fingers to eat his grub. Had he been a Tory, I would have adjusted my aim!

27 July 2011: Shaping Afghan Society

From my missives home, you would have deduced by now that my powers of literacy have their limitations. It will therefore come as a complete surprise for you to learn that my boss has had me drafting letters to a number of important Afghans, including the Minister for something or other.

As one whose preferred writing instrument is a wax crayon, I can tell you now I have had to up my game. Moreover, the letters I drafted had to be translated into Dari, which requires a certain style of wordsmithing. You have to get your point across in a way that is rightly courteous and respectful whilst also being ruthlessly efficient.

I couldn't use complex words, which was an obvious blessing as I don't know any. As my digits poised over the keyboard, I tried to frame my thinking by imagining I was writing to somebody from a profession. The first example that sprung to mind was a politician, but I felt the urge to vent my annoyance, so I binned that.

Then came a barrister, but thoughts of Barbara Williamson in a tutu (Mursley players 2009) swamped my intellectual discourse, so I had to move on. What about a surveyor; don't they respond well to a properly articulated requirement?

Visions of Maggie Coles in the bell tower then loomed in my mind and destroyed any semblance of progress. Finally, I settled on an apparition of Dave Tofield dressed as the Caliph of Jalalabad. This seemed to work, and four letters of dubious quality will be sent winging their way to the translation office. It's funny to think that a combination of the bell tower massive and the Mursley Players may well be shaping the Afghan military, but that's life for you.

28 July 2011: Conducive to Our Fighting Spirit

It was about 01:30 when I was woken from my slumbers by an almighty crash. Fumbling for my pistol, I realised my cellmate was in considerably more distress. After all, it was his bunk that had collapsed.

In an effort to improve the social facility that we Brits have created, somebody had gone to the enormous trouble of creating a montage that hangs proudly on the wall. In effect, it is a large map showing the retreat from Kabul to Jalalabad from 8th-13th January 1842. The individual responsible had painstakingly marked each step of the journey to illustrate where the column of 18,000 was subjected to massacres at the hands of the Afghans.

For those who know their history, the only European to survive was a Dr Brydon, who stumbled into Jalalabad utterly exhausted. By all accounts, two sepoys also made it. As I gazed at this work of art, I was minded to have a word with the morale officer, as I didn't think that this particular composition was conducive to our fighting spirit. However, also marked on the map was the Exfil (extraction of personnel from enemy-occupied terrain). As this was a different route to that shown for 1842, one must presume it was there to inspire confidence in our soldiers that High Command wouldn't make the same mistake twice.

Strapping Lad

He was a strapping lad and rightly proud of his armoured vehicle. I make a point of chatting to our soldiers to show that their officers care. He obviously appreciated it because he asked me if I wanted a lift anywhere. When I suggested that Mursley, Buckinghamshire would be nice, he laughed. Well, he did offer.

A Tax

I have mentioned the challenges of communication where, for many folks, English is their second language. A South American while briefing described that a certain aspect of the Theatre was raising concerns because of "A tax". He was then asked how this tax was manifesting itself. Was money simply being handed over, or was it being taken in kind? He was aghast at this and later pigeonholed me for a quick elocution lesson. Try it yourself . . . A tax . . . attacks. Not easy, is it?

There Isn't as Much as a Globule

I know this will come as a shock to my reader in the Green Man, but there is not a drop of alcohol on the base.

There isn't as much as a globule, bead or drip of the stuff. Even the communion wine is as bereft of this organic compound as an AA convention. Why the labelling on the hand sanitiser almost boasts that it is free of C2 H5 OH. The pursuit of a beer, or a sip of the good stuff, is a fool's errand. There is, however, alcohol-free lager.

However, it is so infused with chemicals that on drinking the stuff, you get a hangover without the booze-induced lift found in the Homme de Vert on a Friday night.

No, I have to report that this is no place for Mursley's sozzled fraternity, and you would just have to content yourself with a glass of distilled germolene, which is root beer. Of course, I don't miss it . . . much.

Five Letters and a Parcel

On plodding to the post room to check for mail, a colleague called over and asked me to check to see if he had had any. Well, he had. Five letters and a parcel.

On the other hand, I had nothing. Not so much as a mess chit. In fact, I haven't had a thing since I arrived, and my regular checks are beginning to induce looks of concern from the postie. I suspect that any day now, this hardened Jock Corporal is going to write me a letter himself.

My slot in the mailroom is gathering dust like a long-forgotten teddy bear. I cheer myself up by telling the soldiers that it's all modern technology nowadays and that there is no place for such old fashion modes of communication as letters. *"Well, of course, sir,"* comes the reply and once again, I depart empty-handed through an honour guard of sympathetic glances.

I was minded to chuck my colleague his parcel. It would have been nice to see the expression on his face. He's a bomb disposal officer.

29 July 2011: I'm the Toilet

She arrived unannounced at the office door, apologising off-handedly for not saluting. I could hardly have been cross as the paying of compliments only applies to Brigadiers and above. All brains and connections this Oxford graduate would hardly have been bothered anyway. Her ilk simply view rank as a minor impediment to their divine right to rule, and right now, she wanted a one-way conversation . . . her way.

She had important people who needed a Theatre-wide assessment of how my particular project was going. I offered her a seat. *"You hadn't wanted this information before, so why the urgency?"*

I knew full well the answer to that. The subject had been neglected, and now all of a sudden, it's number one in the hit parade just as yours truly arrives.

Imagine, if you will, that the military is like your domestic abode. At the sexy end, you have touch-sensitive hobs, granite work surfaces, coffee machines and a 3D television. This is what you show the neighbours.

The military is just like that. Jets, grenade launchers, laser-guided bombs, and high-tech surveillance. This is what they show the politicians. However, there are some things that you would not normally show your neighbours. Take, for example, the toilet. Now go on, admit it. You wouldn't exactly give your friends a guided tour of said appliance. The best that one can expect is "third door on the left". Your toilet is, in fact, a burden. It requires cleaning and involves a routine that polite society just doesn't want to talk about. But all hell breaks loose if it is blocked or is backing up in the bathroom.

This, in rough handfuls, describes my job. I've inherited the military equivalent of the neglected toilet that nobody really cared about. But now it is backing up, and important people think it will make a mess on the floor. This is what I told little Miss Sunshine, albeit not quite like that.

She, however, just wanted me to tell her when I will be able to give her this assessment. I pointed out that a very senior officer had only this morning briefed this issue and that there was very little I could add. This was the brief she hadn't thought necessary to listen to. What price a good education?

So, when you next visit the toilet, gaze fondly at this porcelain necessity. Gently caress the cistern and admire it with a fondness normally reserved for loved ones. I'd appreciate that. I'm the toilet.

30 July 2011: But Not the Dying Eh Prime Minister?

It was the Poles who suffered today. Their flag was at half-mast. The details as to how it happened will have been published on the incident reports. It's much the same story. Dismounted patrol triggers an IED, takes direct fire and evacuates the dead and wounded. Move on. Then a little while later, the same patrol could go through it all again. I cannot claim to have ever been exposed to such horrors, but I have gone through the training and rehearsed the scenarios.

This has given me just a small sense of the totality of terror that the lads are going through. I'm told that the air traffic controllers see the dead and wounded arriving daily. The radio bristles with urgency as our pilots give their all to get these boys as quickly as they can to the hospital. The stretcher-bearers are waiting. Woe betides anybody who gets in their way. They see it as an honour to help these men, and they have no intention of letting them down.

It is almost as if the military has developed terminology to shield itself from the reality of it all.

Cat A means 'limbs missing', Role 3 is a hospital, DOW is 'Died of Wounds', KIA represents 'Killed in Action', and

WIA stands for 'Wounded in Action'. It all amounts to the same thing. The numb inducing shock of a distraught mother being told her son is dead or that he will need 24-hour care for the rest of his life.

These are strong lads. Our medical staff are outstanding. They will survive injuries that only recently would have been fatal. They will then live with those traumas and struggle with what few faculties they have remaining. Frankly, it is awful.

Just imagine for a moment being the mother of an infantry soldier in Afghanistan. Painful isn't it? These mothers live with it, day in and day out.

Or picture, if you will, being an officer back in Britain having to inform a mother that her boy is dead or hurt. I remember being trained to do this. The military describes it as casualty notification training. The instructor gave the class some tips. He finished off by reminding those doing the informing not to break down in tears themselves. Apparently, it is not helpful.

A public figure is alleged to have said recently: *"You do the fighting, I'll do the talking."* I would add to that: *"But not the dying eh Prime Minister?"*

31 July 2011: Compliments to the Chef

Well, there I was on what the American's call a battlefield circulation, visiting an Afghan military base. Our hosts were extraordinarily kind and led us into a cabin where we sat around a long Formica table. Our soldiers were on guard outside, dressed in their Robocop outfits. I was pleased to get my body armour off. I was sweating like a docker's armpit. The weight loss programme was on overdrive that day.

Suddenly there was a flurry of activity, and lunch appeared almost instantaneously. Laid on the table was chopped goat (or lamb), nan bread, piles of rice, roasted chickens and salad. It's strange to be served by a waiter with his thumb in your grub.

The food did, however, look magnificent. We, on the other hand, looked panic-stricken. The western dietary tract is not best placed to accommodate locally cooked food. We had been advised to avoid it. That said it was recognised that such a circumstance would be inevitable. Therefore, we were briefed to steer clear of food that had been washed in water and only select meat that had been well cooked.

I looked at the Generals for leadership, and, to their credit, they tentatively tucked in. It would have been an insult to our hosts not to eat the food. We knew this. We also knew that we had four hours in traffic that afternoon. Six officers in a car with Delhi belly would have been a nightmare. I left the room momentarily to check on the soldiers.

"Do you need some food, lads?," says I.

"No, you're OK, sir," comes the reply.

They, too, had had the training. They did, however, take the Pepsis that I'd brought them. Returning to the lunch, I girded my loins and plunged in.

It was delicious. Utterly, completely and absolutely fantastic. Believe me when I tell you it was by far the best meal I had tasted in ages. Compliments to the chef, I thought. We then got into our cars . . .

August 2011: Look Not Now

Look not now at Britain's dead,
With wars to fight and more ahead.
Have we still to commit our young,
To secure our fuel, our trade, our fun?

Look not now at Britain's dead,
For still we need the foreign bread.
Continue we do to commit our brave,
To secure our homes and the life we crave.

Look you now at Britain's dead,
The names that kept our culture fed.
For foreign fields are from where we feed,
And the best of our young slowly bleed.

01 August 2011: Baby Tank

Every time I leave the base, I recollect the advice given to me by a seasoned Colour Sergeant. His advice was simple: *"Expect to be contacted, and you will not forget anything"*.

I, therefore, launch myself on an unsuspecting Afghanistan wearing my helmet, body armour, ID discs, gloves, ballistic glasses and combat underpants. As if all that isn't enough, I add to the weight with an assault rifle, pistol, morphine, field dressing, tourniquet, 5.56mm ammunition, 9mm ammunition, whistle, map, compass, water, mobile phone and a notebook.

I end up looking like a baby tank. This all seems a bit excessive as I usually then climb into the back of a vehicle. We have our sleeves rolled down, which explains the gloves. In the event of a fire, this should afford a modicum of protection as you make your escape.

Before mounting up, however, we are given a brief. There is now a make of motorcar that I will never be able to look in the bumper again. Once you are in the vehicle, you hear the heavy clunk of the doors closing. Even the pushbikes are armoured around here. You are then cocooned in what is a metal box. If you are claustrophobic, this is no place for you. As you know, I am of small but handsome stature. This has huge benefits as I have room to wriggle.

My colleagues, many of whom are huge beefcakes, are squeezed in like sardines. I always think this is a little unfair because if I have to lug them out in the event of our being hit, it will be a far harder job for me. They will have little trouble on my account. Some of these Americans are so huge they could simply pop me in a pocket.

It seems utterly surreal, driving through Afghanistan and listening to the radio crackle with convoy reports while in the background, the Police hit "Walking on the Moon" hums softly from the car stereo. Then we do a "U" turn. Now, where's my map? This modern satellite stuff is all very well.

02 August 2011: Put Your Training Shoes on

When you go to the gym, you have to take your trainers with you. As you enter, you deposit the shoes that you have been wearing into a locker and then put your training shoes on. This is so that sand and dust isn't then walked throughout the gymnasium. There is a suggestion that some folk find this a bit of a chore. It was reported that one chap walked in carrying a pair of trainers, which he then put directly into the locker and saved himself the trouble of changing his footwear. As he was already wearing a pair, I suppose he figured folk wouldn't notice.

Adopt a Forward Position

The fad for spinning has even arrived in Afghanistan. There is a room set aside that is full of these stationary bikes. As you walk by, the effort exerted by all those people causes a warm wind, rather like a large hairdryer, that flushes its way into the corridor.

There must be, on some occasions, over 40 people on the things. As loud music pumps out into the ether, I adopt a forward position and respond to the demands of our instructor.

Even Lawyers Can Embarrass Themselves

Today a rather unsettled officer complained to me that while going for a shower, nobody had told her that she was in the male washroom.

Her suspicions were aroused when several of them stopped shaving to look at her. They must have thought that Christmas had come early. For reasons of confidentiality, it would be unseemly to say anything more. That said, I cannot resist telling you that even lawyers can embarrass themselves occasionally.

Holding a Dollar Bill

She was dressed in black from head to toe, her burka blown by the traffic as she stood in the centre of the road. Her left hand was aloft, holding a dollar bill. *"What is she doing?,"* I asked.

"Begging," came the reply.

"I should have whipped it out of her hand," said the vehicle commander.

He laughed at the thought of it and then paused, softly saying to himself that that would have been unkind.

Somehow Displaced in Time

The boys were late in getting me. They'd had a tyre shred itself. Normally one would have stopped and changed the wheel, but that was not an option. Lesser men would have seen it as an excuse and turned back, but they were hardened veterans and pressed on at a jogging pace.

When they got to my location, they set about changing the wheel, cursing that their vehicle had let them down. As they did so, my Dutch colleague glanced across at me, and we both stared into the mountains. A thunder rolled towards us. I had heard artillery before on Salisbury plain. But this was different; the mountains magnified the echo, and it was as if they were roaring at me. I felt as if I did not belong. I felt as if I was not only thousands of miles from home but also somehow displaced in time. The growl from the valleys was telling me I had no place here. The Dutchman went to speak. I cut him off.

"They were probably training," I explained. But this was Ramadan. The Afghans would not have eaten or drunk anything during the day. It was early evening; they were therefore unlikely to be practising at this hour. Something

had stirred those metal monsters, and they bellowed their reply.

We drove swiftly back to base. Poverty flying past as I stared through the windows. We were late. Nobody wanted to miss their tea, and the mountains were still howling.

03 August 2011: Paucity of Correspondence

My earlier post about not having received any mail has resulted in my being bombarded by well-meaning friends pointing out that had I left them an address, such a paucity of correspondence would not have occurred. While apologising, I am mindful that had I done so, there would have been a presumption on my part that I would get mail. Knowing the sense of humour that abounds in my circle of buddies, that could have guaranteed the receipt of naff all.

About 90 Hours

Indeed, some folk who I adore have hinted that perhaps I am not as busy as I have let on. Of course, being busy is subjective, but by way of an illustration, the total time last week spent watching TV, going for a walk, chatting in the bar, attending birthday parties, gardening, bell ringing, having a curry, cleaning out my chickens and yelling at the kids was zilch.

Time spent cleaning, physical training, church, writing these jottings, attending to my laundry and phoning home probably ten hours, allowing for sleeping, eating and looking after domestic necessities – it all adds up to a working week (i.e. on task) of about 90 hours. Of course, I am on call for the remaining 78 hours regardless of activity.

You Should All Be Very Proud Of Yourselves

Returning to the subject of mail, it is all rather academic as the post room is now closed for five days for operational reasons (he's off sick!).

I have, however, forwarded the address of my overseas residence to enquirers on other means. I am not minded to do so on this posting as I am still scarred by last year's birthday present.

While it is true that it's the thought that counts, the mankini rather stretched that adage. Hence, I am expecting the worst and will no doubt not be disappointed. I must be the only soldier in Afghanistan terrified of getting mail. You should all be very proud of yourselves.

04 August 2011: Instead She Got Me

The joy of joys the post room has re-opened. And yes, there was sweet Fanny Adam for yours truly. The Corporal was so moved by my plight that he could not contain his emotions and handed me a letter. It was from a member of the public addressed to a soldier out in Afghanistan.

We get quite a few of these, and they are distributed to the troops on an as-needed basis. As I'd been in receipt of squat, I suppose he felt I qualified.

It was a lovely communiqué written by a single girl called Amanda from Scotland. Incredibly kind, it was, however, wasted on me, as I was old enough to be her father. As I read the missive, its charm rising from the page, I could just imagine that as she wrote, she had visions of a stallion of a man striding purposefully across the Afghan plains. His muscular bronze features glistening with the raw strength of an Adonis in his prime. Instead, she got me!

I did, however, write a reply. It was carefully crafted to encourage her to write to "a soldier" again. Hopefully, she will then find a young man with whom she could perhaps strike up a relationship.

I considered her letter a thoughtful act and, in my response, I wished her well. I hope it will not be too much of a let down. It's a cruel sense of fate that Afghanistan should once again see me disappoint a lady.

05 August 2011: Is it Good to Punish a Soldier for a Nation's Guilt?

The Dutch contingent mustered late in the evening to say goodbye to a much-loved Warrant Officer who was rotating out of Theatre. I was also invited along. They were all gutted. He, however, was over the moon. Well, he was at first. He'd been a father figure to most of them, and especially upset was a young Dutch female.

After they had all hugged him, he gathered up his body armour and rucksack and walked to the transport. As he faded into the night, someone called after him. He didn't turn around. It would have been too painful, and his pride wouldn't allow him to show weakness.

Today, he will have learnt from the Dutch press that his former Commanding Officer fears prosecution for his actions at Srebrenica. Perhaps it is good to punish a soldier for a nation's guilt.

06 August 2011: Contents to the General

My mail misfortune has reached a crescendo of humiliation. The poor innocent in all this was the postal NCO. With pride in his profession unsurpassed by our best surgeons, he handed me a parcel.

"Are you sure it's for me?," I asked.

"Absolutely," came the reply.

It was indeed a parcel, and it was indeed for me. My cry of anguish and venting of verbal incoherence was not the response the poor Corporal was expecting. Fate had dealt me a savage blow. Somebody in Satan's sorting office was once again denying me a physical manifestation of home.

To explain, I need do no more than quote to you the content of the letter enclosed within said parcel: *"Hi Lyndon, I hope that this finds you in good spirit. Could you please pass on the contents to the General?"*. No, it did not find me in good spirits, and as for the contents, I could think of exactly where to shove a metal thermal mug and 80 Yorkshire tea bags. Not in the General's direction, I would add, but my predecessor had better watch out.

07 August 2011: The Better Man

He was a bear of a man and towered over me. With a full beard and an AK47 strapped across his chest, he was a fearsome looking fellow. In some ways, he reminded me of an Afghan version of a certain publican who resides in the parish.

I offered him my hand, which he shook without really changing his expression. It felt as if I had engaged with a leg of lamb; such was the size and consistency. His grip paused, surrounding my fingers like a string of Winslow Winners. When he let go, he then almost subconsciously wiped the palm of his hand against his trousers before turning it over to do the back.

While he did so, his deep brown eyes gazed into the distance. It wasn't a powerful grip. It didn't need to be. He had more than made his presence felt. He was a soldier and, from his appearance, most probably a Pashtun. These people have a saying. If you take revenge after a hundred years, it is considered that you have done so too soon. I formed a view very quickly that this was one chap to keep on the right side of.

That said, I and the others were guests of his General. His job was to guard us, and I could imagine what the punishment would be for failure. He may have resented me as a foreigner, or maybe he was nervous about somebody in authority engaging with him. Perhaps he used his physical presence to try and balance the relationship.

Yet I didn't feel threatened, and as the group stepped off, he elected to pace alongside me. When we left, I gave him a wave. He half raised his hand cautiously, as if not to be seen. I could only begin to imagine the life he had led. I have no idea what impression I formed in his mind, but I like to think he understood me as having viewed him as an equal. He could well have been the better man.

08 August 2011: Just have to Make the Best Of It

To keep my reader in the Green Man informed, you may recollect that my cellmate was moving out to alternative accommodation that was more in keeping with his rank.

This he has now done, and from what I can gather, rank doesn't necessarily have its privileges. That said, his going put me back into the Yak Fat School of accommodation management. There was, therefore, a degree of trepidation on my part as to who would be my new cellmate. Well, the other evening, he arrived and frankly, the Mongolian option was looking decidedly the better bet. You heard it here first, but my fellow incarcerant is an RAF officer.

More than that, he is aircrew and therefore doesn't have a normal name like you or me. In keeping with the film Top Gun, he has a "handle", but unlike Top Gun, it is not Maverick, Goose or Slider. He is named after a character from Winnie the Pooh. I am somewhat embarrassed to ask him what his real name is, but I'm sure I'll find it out in due course. Until then, me and "Piglet" will just have to make the best of it.

Notes from the Nocturnal

On the subject of accommodation, we are now in the month of Ramadan, and for those who bunk with those of the Muslim faith, the nights are no longer peaceful. I know little about this great religion but what I have learnt is that during Ramadan, its practitioners rise several times during the hours of darkness to conduct their devotions. For the fellow traveller, this can lead to serious interruptions in one's sleep patterns.

It appears that "Piglet" is not of that calling, so for me, sleep goes on much as usual. However, as I lay there the other night, I did find myself being kept awake by a call to prayer wafting through my mosquito net. These "notes from the nocturnal", while enchanting, did nevertheless remind me of Tim Dolder. He, too, has been denied the joys of a stress-free slumber by religious devotions. Only in his case, I plead guilty, what with my Sunday morning bell ringing an' all.

They say in life that what goes around comes around. For the Pashtun, revenge is a cultural requirement. Well, on that occasion, Tim was certainly getting his own back, albeit vicariously. Tim the "Pashtun". Well, I'm saying nothing, but it might just catch on.

09 August 2011: Lucky

Of all the nicknames that one can acquire in life, "Lucky" has never applied to me. Take, for example, the other day. I'd gone to the church carrying a heavy box containing some toys that I was donating to a charity. As I placed the box down, the Chaplain's assistant helped me unload the assorted goodies. They were destined for some children in Afghanistan.

While unpacking, I suddenly realised that my beret was still upon my head and moreover I was in a chapel. I quickly snatched it off and mumbled an apology. Having then emptied the contents, I lifted the box back up only to then consider putting it back down again.

I needed to do so in order to replace my headdress prior to leaving. Seeing that my accommodation was only some 20 yards away, I decided not to bother. I then stepped briskly forward into the elements exposing my bare bonce as I did so. Now in the British Army, wearing one's uniform outside, without a headdress, is considered a flagrant breach of dress regulations.

Of course, you have to be seen first. Otherwise, technically there is no breach. Unfortunately, I was seen and by a Brigadier of all things. He appeared to ambush me as he emerged from behind an ablution block. Sadly, he wasn't short-sighted and rightly remonstrated with me for my failure to maintain standards. I put the box down promptly, replaced my beret and saluted accordingly. It was, as it happens, a friendly engagement. I say this because as the Brigadier departed, he seemed amused by my circumstance.

Meanwhile, elsewhere in the Theatre, there was an altogether different circumstance. Thirty-eight lads had been killed in a single violent engagement with the Taliban. Maybe I am lucky after all. I will not have to tell their families.

10 August 2011: Loose Wire or Something

Without wishing to alarm anybody, I thought I would give you an update on my experiences of rocket attacks. The first time that such an issue came to prominence was when two Dutchmen in my office were having a heated debate in hurdy-gurdy.

Becoming somewhat distracted, I asked them what the problem was. It seems that from the alarms and sirens, one of them had concluded that we were under rocket attack. The other was saying that this was, in fact, a drill because the email message in front of him said we were going to rehearse such an event. The source of the muddle was one of timing.

The drill was scheduled for earlier in the day, so his colleague assumed that this must therefore be a real attack. By now, I was getting fed up, so I resolved to end the debate once and for all. I suggested that one of them walk outside and find out first hand whether the attack was real or not. This resulted in two dropped jaws, a pair of blank stares and a cessation of the debate. What did I say?

My second encounter was during a video telephone conference that I was leading. All of a sudden, one of the outstations dropped off the screen. A moment later, they reappeared and apologised for the interruption and then explained that they'd just been rocketed. And there was me thinking that it might have been something serious like a loose wire or something.

All That Was Required

From the media reports reaching Afghanistan, it seems that folk in London are having a tough time of things. I found a group of lads simply glued to the TV watching footage of London burning. Thinking I understood soldiers, I was pleasantly surprised by their view that the use of water cannon and plastic bullets was totally unnecessary. In their estimation, all that was required were several sniper teams operating throughout London with orders to identify the ringleaders and shoot them. Crowd dispersal would naturally follow, and folk could then go to bed. They were, I'm sure, only joking, but I did suggest that if called to advise the Prime Minister, they'd run it past Legal first.

11 August 2011: Errant Rounds

If you happen to drop a couple of charged magazines, they make a heck of a noise, especially if the bullets bounce out and roll across the floor. Quite a clatter, in fact. It was this bout of acoustics that woke me in the early hours of this morning. I knew immediately that it was my RAF cellmate preparing for combat.

If in the extremely unlikely event that he gets into a firefight, he will have a cast-iron excuse for having fewer bullets than that with which he was issued. If he doesn't, we may have to completely gut our cell looking for any errant rounds from this morning's spillage. That said, he is not alone in failing to secure one's personal kit.

Mugged a British Soldier

I, too, had a professional lapse when I was mugged by an 11-year-old. I say mugged but "seen off" is probably a better description.

While walking down the street, I was accosted by the little fellow who spoke surprisingly good English. He asked me for a bottle of water, but we are told we mustn't give them anything to avoid encouragement. He soon realised that I was not budging, so he called his mate over, who must have been about eight.

Appealing to my sense of charity and hanging off my shoulder, he then explained that from only one bottle of water, two boys would benefit. My Dutch escort was about as much use as a chocolate fireguard, reminding me that I shouldn't give them anything – but it wasn't him that was becoming the pied piper of Afghanistan.

Fortunately, a bottle of water became exposed, and the little rascal helpfully obtained possession. He stopped, saw I wasn't bothered, and then scampered off. Later in the day, his other mate, obviously figuring I'd lost weight for want of water, offered to sell me a pair of bathroom scales for $1.

I know I'm a bit on the portly side, but I ask you? What did strike me was that my assailant was obviously very intelligent. He could speak English and organise a scenario to his benefit. Hopefully, he'll get an education and make something of himself. Then in 40 years, the President of Afghanistan can boast that when he was eleven, he mugged a British soldier.

As an aside, my dutiful but bored reader in the Green Man may see a small interregnum in my postings. I've to go upcountry for a few days. Apparently, my glamour is needed elsewhere in the Theatre. Back soon . . .

13 August 2011: Thank You

You can stop now. You have made your point. I am no longer the recipient of sympathy and comfort in the post room—no more letters from Amanda for me. A deluge of epistles has swamped my in-tray, and I am now the custodian of bags of the stuff.

I cannot possibly write to thank each individual act of kindness, as the taxpayer believes I am here for other purposes. You are all making me feel quite emotional. I thought that after 27 years in Her Majesty's service that I wouldn't miss mail, but I have to report that that is far from the case. To hold something tangible from home is a real blessing.

Please consider these jottings as a collective thanks to one and all. However, I would like to share some of the contents with you. Whoever sent the toy tanks will be pleased to know that I launched a combined assault on the German's office next door. He manfully stood behind the Belgian as they closed on his position. The fire engine was a very kind gift, but I donated that to a charity.

The height chart was just plain cheeky, but I do get the joke even though the edition of a post-it marking an appropriate waypoint was probably overdoing it. To my reader Phil Poole fishing off the Welsh coast and his lovely wife Carol and daughter Rachael. Can I just say you caused a bit of lower lip wobble?

The picture of the bell tower consequent to Lea Thomson's "amazing grace", and attendant CD, combined nicely with earlier emails on the subject. The photograph of Lea's "bountiful bloom" now adorns my office wall with a lovely composite of Angelina Jolie and I, which I note she has kindly signed on the back. I can't disclose what she says as it is personal.

The two copies of RAF News were a nice touch. Although we are not short of toilet paper out here, I do nevertheless appreciate the gesture. Sadly, the Willy Warmer is several sizes too small, but I am grateful for the thought as the winters can be harsh here about.

The poetry books were an excellent choice and appeal to the academic in me even though the subject matter is light-hearted. The parish magazine is also welcome, although Garry Lee Sumvill is slipping of late. My birthday presents from the outlaws will remain unopened until the big day (05 September) despite the advice from my Dutch colleague who said they'd never know. *"Don't you believe it?"* was my reply.

When a gentleman with whom I am but an occasional acquaintance goes to the trouble of writing an endearing letter, I conclude that maybe I'm not such a rough fellow after all. It must have been a female who sent me the "man flu" mints, as only a man really understands the awfulness of that affliction. I may be making light of these many kindnesses, but they do mean an awful lot . . . thank you.

14 August 2011: Doors to Manual

If ever you find yourself climbing into a US Army Blackhawk helicopter and have an aversion to heights, don't go for a window seat. I could have done with this tip before I purposefully strapped myself in and waited for the doors to manual piece.

Unfortunately, there were no doors to manual. In fact, there were no doors at all, and as we rose majestically into the vertical, I could see Afghanistan in all its glory by my left foot. The cabin crew who were by now manning two pintle-mounted machine guns had thought it unnecessary to close said doors. I have seen enough war films to know that this might have been the case, so it shouldn't have come as a surprise.

One of the reasons why earlier in my career, I volunteered for sea service was to avoid the Army sending me up mountains and putting me in a paraffin parrot, neither of which I find particularly appealing. I must congratulate the Army because, on this occasion, it managed both.

Not only was I in a helicopter, but the helicopter was flying through the mountains of Eastern Afghanistan. If that wasn't bad enough, the pilot seemed to see a reason to occasionally bank the aircraft leaving me almost face down. At that point, I was rather glad that the cabin crew was servicing the machine guns because if they'd given me a coffee, I'd have spilt it, and my peanuts would have gone everywhere.

The landing was, as you'd expect, a simple pleasure, and my pace towards the waiting transport was somewhat unseemly.

Professional Capacity

As we cruised along, our driver struck up a conversation. It must be my accent. As a soldier, she is part of a mortuary affairs company, and last week's Chinook incident had kept her busy. Coincidently her first-ever tasking was some years ago when she had to attend to a trooper killed in a helicopter crash in Iraq. She was reassuringly professional in the description of her work, and I was confident that matters would have been attended to with great reverence.

When she returned my colleague and I to the airhead, I said cheerio and told her that it was nothing personal, but I hope I didn't meet her in a professional capacity. She laughed at my remark, although she hadn't laughed earlier. Subsequent to her tour in Iraq the incident had caused her problems, and she'd needed help in order to come to terms with it.

Hardly surprising, really, as she was only eighteen at the time. So was the dead soldier; God bless him.

15 August 2011: Excellent Anglican Vintage

As the Afghan doctor bent over me and inserted a needle the size of an exhaust pipe into my right arm, it felt much like home. He, too didn't have English as a first language.

I'd volunteered to give blood to the local hospital. I say "to" and not "at" as that would have been an altogether different experience. It hurt more than in the UK and took longer despite my squeezing a rubber ball like a prize-fighter.

Just like in the UK, the processing included documentation that required me to respond to a number of personal questions. One of the questions asked was if I'd had diarrhoea in the last two months. This is Afghanistan, so that was affirmative, as it was for most people.

I undertook this act of benevolence for two reasons. Firstly, a former Salvation Army trombone playing English doctor asked me to, and secondly, there is a desperate shortage of blood in this country. When an Afghan goes to the hospital for planned surgery, he or she is expected to provide his or her own blood.

This will either have been sourced in the bazaar, or relatives rock up on the day to help out. I can now claim to have spilt blood in Afghanistan. One pint of finest Anglo Saxon of excellent Anglican vintage is now sitting in a blood bank in Kabul. Meanwhile, I've got an arm like a 40Ib car jack. There will be no repetition.

16 August 2011: I Can Do Squalor

If my reader in the Green Man is eating, I advise him to read no further as I am returning to the well-worn subject of ablutions.

I feel I have to if for no other reason than to have a go at sewage engineers and all those who design and build toilet blocks. It's not that I'm averse to muck. I have slept in a shell scrape, a fire trench, in the rain and in the woods. I have bathed naked standing in a washing up bowl, used deep trench latrines, desert roses, turdises and all the panoply associated with an Army in the field.

Ladies and gentlemen, I can do squalor. But what I can't do is a shoddily built facility pretending to be a preferable alternative to a good old-fashioned shovel and a hole in the ground.

Let me explain. I was a guest of the Americans staying in what could be described as transit accommodation consisting of plywood huts and the now much-maligned toilet block. I have three criteria when I am with my fellow male ablutors. Put simply, I do not want to see it, smell it or hear it. This facility failed catastrophically on all three counts.

125

Consisting of a container with aluminium partitions and shower curtains for doors, the ensemble was topped off with continental toilets. Without wishing to be too explicit, these are where the downpipe is at the front of the toilet rather than in the rear as per that excellent design by Thomas Crapper. This continental variant coupled with the effects of institutional feeding means that on flushing, the sailors are not sent to sea and are thus left there by the soldiery grinning inanely at the subsequent user.

I have enquired as to who the lunatic was who designed said abomination and was informed that it was to allow the depositee to inspect for worms. Well, it was all too much for me. I hold my bodily waste in too high a regard to subject it to that filth. Moreover, I am now completely in sympathy with my German colleague, who is going through the gender reassignment process. After that experience, the thought crossed my mind that soon this officer would no longer have to be in the company of males during their morning constitution.

Recently I fell into conversation with the said Lieutenant Colonel who was utterly charming.

17 August 2011: Negligent Discharges

I like my pistol because it is small and light. I like my assault rifle because it is a lot more effective. I was once told that a pistol is a great weapon until somebody is shooting at you.

Being weapons, they do, of course, require loading. As we leave the base, we are reminded to do so. For my pistol, I insert a magazine into the handgrip, and for my assault rifle, I do likewise into the magazine housing. Before doing so, however, I will have checked the sights, that the safety catch is on and that the change leaver is set to semi-automatic.

When we return, we have to do the reverse and unload our weapons. For the pistol, a simple button discharges the magazine. That done, you then bring the working parts to the rear to check that the chamber is empty.

On doing this, you tilt the weapon on to its side so that any round would fall out, and then you inspect the chamber. If the chamber is clear, you release the working parts forward. Now with a Browning pistol, you still have to release the trigger mechanism. If you have a long middle finger, you simply place it where the magazine was and release it accordingly.

If you have a stumpy digit, this is not possible, so you have to reapply the magazine in order to do so. In training, you would have an empty magazine with which to do so as nobody likes to put a charged magazine back on the weapon and then pull the trigger. On operations, however, you'd be an idiot for carrying an empty magazine just for that purpose.

Back in goes the live magazine, and when pointing the pistol into the unloading bay, you complete the evolution. If you have got it wrong, then there is a big bang, and life becomes considerably unpleasant as you expect to be charged.

With the assault rifle, the principles are the same. Only it is a little more complex. Again, you bring the working parts to the rear in order to see into the chamber. You look forward, back and down. You pass your hand underneath to check the magazine is not still attached, and then you again check the chamber. Once you are satisfied, you release the working parts forward and squeeze the trigger.

In some places, an NCO will check as you do this. To finish you apply the safety catch, check the change leaver is set to semi-automatic and replace the dust cover. All very simple, straight forward and very necessary. If you have not done these drills properly, then there is a good chance that when cleaning your weapon, you will fire off a round.

This has happened, normally in one's accommodation. The bullet will pass through the wall and could well strike a colleague. Although his singing along to The Black Eyed Peas on his iPod may suggest he deserves it, you will nonetheless make yourself extremely unpopular. If you have not switched the change leaver from automatic to semi-automatic and also left the magazine on, being unpopular will be the least of your worries.

Now, of course, these drills are simple. However, when you are an eighteen-year-old who is hungry and completely and utterly chin strapped, having just seen his mate killed, things are no longer so straight forward. This sort of circumstance is why I can understand how negligent discharges can happen, but the poor Afghan who was shot on base this week as a result of such an incident may think differently. If, of course, he hadn't Died of Wounds (DOW).

18th August 2011: Job Offers Anyone?

It may be because of my good looks, but I'm finding that the frequency with which I am off base visiting senior Afghans has gone up. I don't go on my own, of course, but invariably accompany a general; sometimes more than one.

The offices are of a tired appearance with furniture of Middle Eastern design that tries to look grand. Regularly, there are flowers, a picture of President Karzai and an Afghan flag. The rug, however, is always impressive. The Afghans are extremely courteous, and as it is Ramadan, they are also extremely apologetic about not being able to provide anything to drink.

In respecting their culture, we also do not sip from our water bottles, so I tend to stock up a bit before I go in. This would have been a great tactic but for my inefficient bladder. At the first meeting, I ended up crossed-legged, praying for the fire alarm to go off, so I could make an exit via the loo. This was a distinct possibility as gazing at the TV, I noticed the plug arrangement was a simple connect of two wires from the TV with two wires emerging from a hole in the wall.

The connection appeared to be achieved by sellotape, but regardless of that, it would certainly have given "Jet Set" a bit of a turn. I also noticed, rather reassuringly, a fire engine parked at the entrance of the building within which I was occupying the top floor.

At these meetings, I was at first unsure as to what particular brand of fairy dust I was supposed to be sprinkling. I soon cottoned on mind . . . take notes. I took this upon myself as nobody else seemed to bother, and in my reckoning, there were folks there who were paid to do just that. Now, remember we are talking Dari to English via an interpreter, some of whom are in the habit of whispering. Moreover, this information has then to be processed through my limited faculties to produce a piece of work, which contributes to our supporting the Afghans.

There are, of course, the obvious pooh traps, and as I blindly clicked on the spell checker, I noticed that my misspelling of the word "guest" offered up "gusset" which would have certainly been a source of embarrassment. I have to say, without being overly modest, that I'm brilliant at this. Indeed, one officer returning to the USA asked for a copy of my work to use as a template for instructing his students.

The pity of it all is that this brilliance is perhaps wasted on the Army, which is considering making me redundant, and I should perhaps be applying it elsewhere . . . job offers anyone? Of course, this modesty could come a cropper should I have one of my spell checker episodes.

19th August 2011: We've Got a Consultant Out Here

I don't know who it is yet, but I think we've got a consultant out here. My suspicions were aroused when somebody mentioned the word re-organisation. I use that term in its loosest sense because what they really meant was job cuts.

Each department has been told to cut a given number of posts. This sounds all very Soviet to me. I would have expected an approach that involved mapping the requirement against the available manpower, their skill sets and what the forecast change in workload is likely to be. We could clearly do with Alex Gallon out here, but I suspect he would find the working conditions somewhat disagreeable, as there's no lager.

We have to cut posts on a numerical basis but still, nevertheless, have to identify impacts in order to support the measures. My Dutch colleague offered up his position. When I asked to see the underpinning work, he said there wasn't any, but it would mean him going home, which was the only intellectual justification he needed. Not a lot you can say to that, really. All in all, he's not been having the best of times lately.

A young Dutch officer charged with organising all their R&R flights expressed concern that he didn't have contact email addresses for all the Dutch folk, so my oppo kindly said he'd sort it out for him. This he did only to discover that his kind gesture was rewarded by him, and only him, being left off the flight manifest.

He wasn't happy and then complained that he couldn't resign because he didn't know to whom he should submit his resignation. He'd gone from the Dutch Navy to NATO and is now here. His immediate boss is me, an Englishman, my boss is an American, his boss is a Pole, and his boss is a Frenchman, and then we are back to the Americans again. I said I'd accept his resignation if he would accept mine, but that, of course, will get us nowhere. I think he's gone off to write to his MP now.

20th August 2011: No More Willy Warmers

I know that winter is coming because the old QM has asked me to complete a demand form outlining the clothing that I want. Now, if it is the desert pattern Gore-Tex jacket, I think I'm out of luck. As my tour includes the winter, I should have deployed with it anyway, although it will have been in the woodland pattern, so I'd look like an oak tree. Well more a shrub considering my altitudinal qualities.

There are boots, but the QM has suggested that not everyone needs them and that when I go home on R&R, I should collect my old boots and bring them out here. Arctic socks, windproof over-trousers, and arctic mittens are all available, but again, they are all in the woodland pattern. There are some softie jackets but likewise also in short supply. Like the other clothing, they come in any colour provided it's green. The more appropriate multi-terrain pattern temperate issue softie is not yet available.

All of the above is caveated by the not insignificant observation that the boys in the forward operating bases and those in the dismounted role will have priority. This, of course, is right and proper, but I submitted my demand anyway. Worry not I'll be fine, so please no more willy warmers and the like as I have made provision. The original article is hanging on my office wall. The American Chief of Staff asked me what it was, and I told him that it was an example of British Army winter issue clothing. My lederhosen colleague, I think, has cottoned on.

Well, it seems nothing changes in the Army regarding kit. In the rear without the gear. So, if you see an excited botanist on a BBC news report, having spotted a shrub above the snowline in Afghanistan, do dismiss it out of hand. It is highly likely to be me.

21st August 2011: Say My Prayers and Trust in My Body Armour

You will have seen it in the news. The fighting was vicious. In terms of proximity, if I was centred on the Green Man, it all happened within the parish.

Rip-Van-Robinson, however, slept through it all. I sometimes wonder what it will take to wake me up. When I was at sea, a simple change in engine revolutions had me on the bridge in an instant. In Iraq, one large bang and the boy was mobile. But not yesterday.

Folks were desperately trying to stay alive, and I slept soundly on, oblivious, away with the fairies, ensconced in the land of nod. My colleague heard the fighting and a Dutch policeman claims to have felt the pressure wave. I felt nothing, and had I done so, I would have attributed it to the food. Some soldier I am!

When I arose and bimbled off to Church, the talk was of nothing else. The Padre didn't show up. This was eminently sensible as travelling around on Afghan Independence Day would be unwise, especially if you were an Englishman. We Brits appeared to be the target, and I laughed as an American shuffled away from me.

I note with interest the Prime Minister describing the attack as cowardly. While it is perhaps not for me to comment, I would argue that a ground assault coupled with the certainty of death is not the act of a bunch of cowards. Our soldiers are not up against cowards; were that only true. They are up against ruthless killers who care not for their own, their people and certainly not for us. Behind my fortification, I feel quite safe, but I do sense death in the way one senses goodwill at Christmas. I don't think about it. Twenty-seven years in the Army has taught me that the absence of the normal is the presence of the abnormal. If it doesn't look right, it isn't right. I say my prayers and trust in my body armour.

22nd August 2011: Ended up Like a Hamster

Fortifications and I do not get along. As you would expect, there is an element of protection out here, and some of it is quite elaborate with passageways, turnstiles, heavy doors and all sorts.

In fact, it is so elaborate that at one location, I walked in off the street only to find my Dutch colleague chasing after me because I was walking straight back out again. He'd wised up to my limited faculties earlier on when I'd attempted to transit one of the turnstiles.

Whoever designed it must have used the dimensions of an anorexic because it was so narrow I doubt Kate Moss could have got through it. Moreover, it is completely enclosed, so there is no climbing over or under. Basically, it's a small spoked enclosed horizontal wheel that rotates to allow folk to pass. It was into this instrument of incompetence that I launched myself tooled up in my Robocop ensemble.

The opening few steps were no problem, but then I found that my manly chest, entombed as it was in body armour and pouches, was too wide for access. If that wasn't bad enough, my rifle seemed to have fed itself between several bars of the wretched contraption, and my ammunition grab bag completed my misfortune by hooking itself around some other part of the instrument.

All in all, it was a sorry sight, and I ended up like a hamster in one of those Ferris wheels you see in their cages. The flying Dutchman came to my rescue by first attempting to push me back through it and then trying to shove me forward. It was like an episode out of Dad's Army with my playing the part of Captain Mainwaring with a Dutch Sergeant Wilson. The Macedonians were now starting to take an interest, no doubt, figuring out how to explain their capture of a British Army Lieutenant Colonel. I eventually extricated myself despite the Dutchman's efforts by peeling off my kit and then dragging it through after me. I wouldn't say it was humiliating rather, it was plain annoying.

Of course, I'm British, and we walk. The yanks drive, and it is highly likely I was the first to ever try and negotiate said contrivance in full kit. I'll not be doing it again, that's for sure.

23rd August 2011: I Can't Get Enough Of Charles Dickens

Shakespeare has come to Afghanistan. I became aware of this cultural excursion from posters around the base. It had clearly caused a degree of excitement because the subject was raised in one of our morning meetings. Hamlet, to be precise. My being English, like the play write, obviously created an expectation that somehow I'd be interested.

"I'm a great fan of Hamlet," said I to a now intrigued audience.

"In fact, I find all of those Elizabethan plays utterly fascinating".

By now, I had them hooked and concluded my spiel with the comment: *"I can't get enough of Charles Dickens."*

I'm not sure that the Americans have worked out my sense of humour. The General smiled, although several others looked embarrassed for me. Anyhow it was proposed that several of us go along, including me.

As you know, my understanding of high culture is settling down with a packet of cheese and onion and a pint of real ale while listening to my friend Dave Tofield belt out "My Way" on his karaoke.

This, however, was an altogether different experience. The play was being delivered by the one actor, who is serving out here as a mobilised United States Navy Reservist. He played to a packed house.

On arriving with the General I did wonder where on earth we were going to sit. I needn't have worried. You can rely on the Germans. My German friend had already been in and reserved the best seats. Not with bathing towels mind but with some place names he'd used at a meeting. I took the Michael accordingly but was grateful for his efforts. The actor played 12 parts using only a book and a cardigan as props.

While I agree it was an abridged version, and therefore only lasted two hours, it was nevertheless brilliant. Something is rotten in the state of Denmark. Or did he actually say Afghanistan?

24th August 2011: I Love You English

In some ways, it is like home here. We, too, get nuisance phone calls. My caller is a young boy who I'd say is about in his mid-teens. On occasions, he phones me up.

"Talk English," he demands down the phone. The line then goes dead, and after a pause, the phone rings again. *"I love you English,"* he then says and once again hangs up. The third call is his Coups de Graz when he shouts *"Taliban!"* down the phone and finishes his banter off in a fit of laughter.

It really is funny, and I'm beginning to look forward to his calls. However, now when the phone rings, and I think it's him, I get my Dutch colleague to answer in hurdy-gurdy. He, too, then bursts out laughing as the lad can't make head or tail of it. It's an unfunny thing what war can do to kids; what with them making nuisance calls or being a ten-year-old up dressed up in a suicide vest and then sent out to die.

25th August 2011: GROTB Option

I could never live with myself were I to learn that soldiers in the field were suffering because of inaction on my part. This is not a unique quality. It is prevalent throughout the officer corps of the British Army.

But the question I am now asking myself is, does that also apply to soldiers who are not of my army? You and I know the answer to that, but things are never that simple. If I leave those responsible to simply get on with it, then no harm can be done in the long term, but in the short term, folk in the field will continue to suffer. That distress will carry on until such times as certain individuals decide to pull their finger out.

If I get positively medieval with people, which I have to confess is occasionally my style (I think they call it small man complex), then I could ruin future relationships. Whilst I found the "Get Rid Of The B***ard" option tempting, I'm just going to have to be a little more patient. Of course, patience is relative. Waiting for loved ones to get in the car perhaps a minute. Waiting for loved ones to clean the car perhaps a decade (and counting!).

I'm going to give this particular issue a few days, after which it's the GROTB option.

Death Is a Second-Order Issue

This, though, is a minor impediment compared to a colleague's predicament. He was struggling with an issue of conscience and explained that the tragedy was that folk were getting killed.

That, however, was not a show stopper. It was, in terms of the mission, a second or third-order hindrance. It was not the primary concern, and it was the primary concern to which we needed to turn our attention. It is strange to operate in a world where death is a second-order issue.

In the UK, it would shut a factory. If it involved UK citizens, the embassies would erupt. Out here, someone may get some paperwork.

26th August 2011: Cock-up in the Big House

Big disappointment in Afghanistan. The Royal Marines' band had set up to entertain the troops, and folks had taken their seats. I'd secured for myself a front-row position, having considered myself on this occasion a VIP. It became clear that all was not well after a reported delay of ten minutes soon elapsed with no subsequent harmonies wafting through the air.

Presently a burly Sergeant stood up and announced it was off; the show was cancelled; thank you all for coming along. There was a ripple of applause, and that was it. The crowd dispersed. It was the best rendition of "Silent Night" in British military history.

Rumours swept the compound. High Command had cancelled it for fear of offending the Afghans during their holy month of Ramadan. The Royal Marine band had put themselves at some risk to get here (remember Deal?), and the troops were chuntering.

Something had gone badly wrong. A cock-up, not so much in the cookhouse, but in the big house. It's certainly strained relations with our American cousins. After their belting out country and western last Thursday evening, it was assumed the coast was clear. That said, it is highly likely High Command was unaware of this previous racket; otherwise, that too would have been given the order of the boot. Generals are never required to justify their decisions to their subordinates, but the decision-maker is required to personally convey bad news. That this did not happen is a source of regret. And I'm sure the lads' mags left lying about the place is not a source of offence to the Afghans, but do not start me off on the customs and culture of a NATO Army in the field.

27th August 2011: Surely, He Had a Wheelchair?

He clenched me by the arm. It was a surprisingly strong grip, like a sailor hauling you from a long boat. I looked down. He had a muscular torso and arms more normally associated with a gymnast.

His legs, however, were like twisted vines bent and useless under his bottom. I'd seen him moments earlier propelling himself across the road using his arms like paddles. He had no wheelchair. His ambulatory mechanism consisted of what looked like a boy's go-cart.

I'd noticed the traffic and remembered thinking, how was I going to push the cart clear of the large 4x4 bearing down on him? I needn't have worried. He was up on me in an instant with the cart bouncing over the kerb. It was twilight, and I wanted to get back to base. Darkness was settling in quick. He spoke. I shook him off. He followed. My oppo said something about begging.

"He must have a wheelchair, surely?" I said.

"That cart is horrendous".

"It adds to the effect," came the reply. I am not so sure. He managed the cart too well. He was obviously very accustomed to it. Maybe it suited him more than a chair. Surely, he had a wheelchair? He was a young man in his early twenties. The police didn't mind him. Maybe he was one of their numbers crippled in war service. He called after me. I walked on.

He then shouted. He sounded angry, his voice trailing off in the dark. I felt awful. Hardening your heart is a tough business, but there are limbless everywhere. You can choke on the weight of it all. Somebody else to add to my prayers.

28th August 2011: Not Going by Horse?

I am very proud of the skill of arms badge on my uniform that tells the Army I'm an Ocean Watchkeeper and hence a navigator. Well, it's coming off tomorrow. Somebody gave me a map and a radio and made me a vehicle commander in a convoy that was required to transit the city.

The most dangerous thing in the British Army is an officer with a map, and I am no exception. The plaintive cries that I'm used to charts cut no ice. The only blessing was that I was in the following vehicle. Mind you; it could have been worse; I could have been made the driver.

As with any move, there was a detailed brief. This is the route, this is who has got what equipment, and this is how the radio works. Here are all the natures of pyrotechnics, and there is a bottle of water in the back. The sneaky beaky device is as follows, and you'll be using that.

That was all very well, I thought, but where is the magic button? This is what I press when it all goes horribly wrong to summon the cavalry. Once I knew where that was, I was decidedly happier.

My driver was a French Canadian, and I'd already upset him having slaughtered his first language. Well, you've got to seize every moment to practice. Another Canadian was driving the lead vehicle in the back of which sat a Canadian Mountie. *"Not going by horse?"* I thought but didn't dare say it.

We set off. My eyes pinned to the map and the vehicle in front. I thought the last little nugget about checking for magnetic mines being placed against the side of the car when stuck in traffic, was a real morale booster.

Let me tell you; it was some manoeuvre. There appear to be no traffic regulations. Folk seem to select their direction of travel regardless of the evident flow. You thus frequently find cars coming towards you in the same lane. Flocks of goats, carts, pedestrians and several lunatics on a pushbike all add to the hazards. Kids as young as six meandering about, old folk, young folk and donkeys laden with goods all add to this tyranny of the tarmac.

I was glad when it was all over. The overall packet commander knew his job. In fact, he impressed the heck out of me. Well, what do you expect from a Grammar schoolboy and an Aylesbury Grammar schoolboy at that? As we motored through the dusty, crowded and busy streets, thoughts turned to the annual humiliation when the John Colet 15 was beaten by him and his ilk. I'd been part of the losing team more times than I can remember. But it would have been rather foolish to get my own back today.

29th August 2011: An Excellent Alternative to Organised PT

The increase in the number of British Soldiers going sick on base with diarrhoea was naturally a source of concern. I enquired of the Sergeant as to what he thought the problem was. Is it the cookhouse, or are the lads just not washing their hands enough?

"Most likely cause, sir?" he said. *"The pretty new medic in the med centre."*

By all accounts, she is real honey, and the lads are coming up with all sorts of complaints in order to get to see her. I think that the large Mongolian with the shaven head is a medic. I shall see if he shouldn't be reassigned.

Other dodges include munching on garlic. The theory is that if you stink enough, the boss will not hang around, thus limiting his capacity to assign more work. It's a novel approach and reassuring to see that the soldiery is ever creative. I stumbled across a gaggle of them sat around the TV watching a group of bikini-clad women exercising on a beach.

I think it's shown once a week on the British Forces Broadcasting Service. The programme may be Australian in origin or Californian or something but what I will say is the coastal scenery was certainly enchanting. I looked at the Corporal and asked him what he thought the merits were in this particular programme.

Several pairs of eyes looked up at me from the couch as he began to explain. They didn't have a physical training instructor deployed with them, and as a caring section commander, he was conscious of this. To that end, he had therefore identified this programme as an excellent alternative to organised PT. Sometimes it is appropriate to just thin out. This occasion was one of them

30th August 2011: Enough Movement From the Food

The bloke looked quite happy as he bounced his motorcycle over the mudded ruts at the side of the road. For the woman on the back dressed in a burka, I suspect she felt decidedly different, what with clutching a baby an' all. It is easy to see how horrific injuries can happen, especially as people cruise down the road at 40mph hanging on to the side of vehicles. Accidents happen frequently.

I was asked to join a number of Christians in seeing the consequences of such at the local hospital. I declined; partly because I travel only when it is necessary, and secondly, I don't think I was emotionally configured for such an event.

I saw the Chaplain when he came back. They'd gone to the burns' unit of all things. He had the look of a man totally unprepared for what he'd seen. He had broken down in tears. The torment of a young girl having proved too much for him. He was so moved he told us that he'd had an overwhelming urge to hold her hand and pray over her.

In my view, this was a decidedly unwise thing to do in a devout Muslim country. The Chaplain related that as he did so, the girl's eyes welled with tears in acknowledgement. As if she knew full well what he was doing. I think he had a life-changing experience similar to when I met some young boys in the Balkans who'd had their testicles shot away by Serb paramilitaries. I'm glad I hadn't gone with him and the others, but in my heart, I know I should have. I do not want to be moved by another person's pain. I get enough movement from the food, thank you.

31st August 2011: Bard of the Bathroom Epistle

Regular readers of Open Gates will be delighted to learn that Lyndon Robinson has made a guest appearance in Afghanistan. In order to entertain themselves, these rough, tough and hardened men of the sword organised a poetry evening.

Yes, you read it correctly . . . a poetry evening. Well, naturally, this bard of the bathroom epistles just had to join in. I read three of my own efforts and "In Memoriam" by Ewart Mackintosh.

Now there is, at least if you are an American, a protocol to these sorts of events. When the first soldier-poet finished, I thought his work was really good and clapped accordingly. I soon learned that one does not show approval by clapping. One shows appreciation by clicking one's fingers. I felt a prize wally, but being English, no doubt got away with it. I was taken by the subject matter covered, which included social problems in the USA.

Apparently, 70 per cent of American prisoners lack a father figure, and this social ill seems to feed abuse, child poverty, drug-taking and other social ills. I was impressed that these young soldiers were so socially aware that my opening couplet of "Kill the Taliban, that evil man" had perhaps completely misread the gravity of such an event. Yes, I am joking!

They have invited me back to another event next month, and as I seem to be light on other social engagements at the moment, I have accepted.

September 2011: Military Redundancy

Lose your life or your livelihood,
The Queen's shilling did you no good.
No contract or union to protect your employment,
For you trusted in a Military Covenant.
Well, it failed you, and now you're out.
To tout your wares in a jobseekers' drought.

The MoD said you were a public servant,
Shame you weren't a fêted consultant.
For thousands, a day is what they can earn,
With unlimited liability of no concern.
Well, MoD failed you, and now you're out.
To tout your wares in a jobseekers' drought.

On scarlet benches, old Generals will snore,
A boring debate in the House of Guffaw.
On park benches, redundant Tommies will sleep,
Broken minds their company to keep.

Well, you trusted in donkeys yet again,
Will you never learn, you lions of men?

1st September 2011: We Do Ask a Lot of Our Soldiers

My regular reader in the Green Man has expressed doubts as to an earlier posting that referred to the phenomenon in Afghanistan of "man love Thursday".

I hope folk viewed those comments as simply an expression of humour rather than any social comment on my part. The bottom line, however, is that I am not making it up. I have done a little research. Not too much, I might add, as the subject is of little interest to me. However, the following is a redacted extract from an unclassified source:

In XXXX, British Marines returning from an operation deep in the Afghan mountains spoke last night of an alarming new threat—being propositioned by swarms of gay local farmers. An Arbroath Marine, XXXX XXXXXXXX, said: *"They were more terrifying than the al-Qaeda. One bloke who had painted toenails was offering to paint ours. They go about hand in hand, mincing around the village.'*

While the Marines failed to find any al-Qaeda during the seven-day Operation XXX, they were propositioned by dozens of men in villages the troops were ordered to search.

Another Marine in his 20s stated: *"It was hell . . . Every village we went into, we got a group of men wearing make-up coming up, stroking our hair and cheeks and making kissing noises."*

I was speechless. Well, I was when I'd recovered from a bout of humour. To paraphrase Rudyard Kipling: *"Well, it's Tommy this and Tommy that and Tommy go away, but it's thank you, Mr Atkins when the boys come out to play."*

We do ask a lot of our soldiers.

2nd September 2011: Not Been Selected For Redundancy

I was told last month that on the 1st of September I would get a phone call informing me as to whether or not I'd been made redundant. However, I shouldn't worry, as I will not be because I am on operations. Unless, of course, I have volunteered in which case I may, or I may not be. Yesterday I received the phone call:

"I am phoning to notify you that you have not been selected for redundancy, but this does not mean you will not be selected in the future."

Servicemen and women like me will have received similar calls across the Theatre. We can now all breathe a sigh of relief and go back to the job at hand, which is to get Afghanistan back on its feet while trying to keep our soldiers alive. Of course, the fact that we may lose our jobs in the future will have no adverse impact on our professional drive to undertake these tasks.

After all, it would be very selfish of us not to recognise that the United Kingdom is desperately short of money. Those service personnel being sacked back in the UK can take real pride in this final act of service to their country.

There can be no nobler an undertaking than to lose your livelihood to fund such worthy causes as bailing out the banks, increasing contributions to the European Union and bombing Libya.

Not to mention that wonderful sporting event called the Olympics with its expensively priced tickets for those who are short of a bob or two.

Nonetheless, it does all seem rather harsh, and it may ease troubled souls to know who is responsible. However, considering the laudable aims of getting sacked to save money for these more worthwhile purposes, how can any soldier ever really object to losing his living on such a noble account?

3rd September 2011: Beautiful English Need Beautiful Thing

I loathe shopping. Always have done. Identify what you need and where it is. Go and buy. No mission creep, just get what you require and get out. This is my shopping philosophy, and my tolerance is about fifty minutes.

In Afghanistan, it is about five minutes. He tugged at my arm.

"You English?" he inquired.

He then leant forward, his wares spread across a table, and whispered:

"You English, I charge ten dollars, you American, I charge 20 dollars."

Here we go, I thought the classic Afghan shakedown.

"But I have very little money," I responded.

He then changed tack and asked if I had shampoo. Shampoo! What on earth would I be doing walking around with a bottle of shampoo? He went on and explained that it was very expensive. I looked at his hair. It was thick and lush, albeit in the Saturday Night Fever style. It could, I suppose, have done with washing. I explained that I had no shampoo, so the subject returned to money. *"OK, I have a little,"* I said, a bracelet now being tied to my wrist.

"You English, I love you English, something for your woman," he entreated.

Then I made my mistake and told him I had three, a wife and two daughters.

"Beautiful English need beautiful thing."

Suddenly a necklace and a second bracelet were proffered, presumably the necklace for my wife and the bracelets for my girls. I was in it now, and full well knew it. I proffered some dollars. He looked at my other pockets.

"Look pockets other money," he helpfully advised.

This was true and out came a clump of Euros. I claimed with a degree of honesty that this was all I had. He accepted the offering, satisfied no doubt that I'd been suitably fleeced. My girls, on my return, will now receive a little something from this encounter. They'd better say they like them even if they don't. I went through commerce's answer to Saddam Hussain to get them.

4th September 2011: Expect to be Clamped

In our country, when you park illegally, you can expect to be clamped. It is no different here. As I bimbled off to breakfast, I noticed that a vehicle was in the sure embrace of such a device courtesy of the International Military Police.

It is no secret to tell you that in military establishments, under certain threat levels, you are not allowed to park a car against a building that is occupied by people. This is for the obvious reason that if it contains a bomb, there is an increased risk of death or injury. So I suppose if you have clamped it, that makes it alright then?

No, I didn't think so. That said, as it was an armoured vehicle, I suppose the police knew full well it was one of ours and just wanted to make a point. I thought this was a bit harsh until I realised the truck was German, which gave it a nice touch. Moreover, this suggested to me that our two Dutch police officers were on duty last night. They are very efficient and, of course, have long memories.

After Zee War

It is not true to say that the Germans lack a sense of humour. My Dutch colleague, on seeing a German Colonel, offered a compliment by raising his arm at a right angle to the elbow. With his palm facing outwards, he did not get the chance to complete the manoeuvre by moving his hand from side to side. The German said: *"In zee German Army, vee stopped saluting like that after zee war."*

The Dutchman had only meant to wave.

Very Tasty

Later the same Dutchman had a bout of the giggles. I have not had his story confirmed, but apart from the clamping incident, the German's have had another disappointment.

At great expense, they had trained a number of dogs in the security role and accordingly bequeathed them to an Afghan unit. On returning to the said unit, they enquired of the Afghans if they'd liked the dogs. The Afghans responded that they did, very tasty in fact.

Speechless With Joy

I arrived at the post room on the off chance there might be something for me. The postie filled a mail sack with parcels.

"Somebody's got a birthday," he announced as I pondered how to get it back to my cell. It was, as we say in the trade, an "ugly load" as I sought to balance it over my shoulder. I felt conspicuous as I laboured to move it across the position. Folk would smile as I walked by, thinking I must be the new post boy. That was all a few days ago. Today on the eve of my 50th birthday, I opened them. I know I should have waited, but I've a busy day tomorrow. I'm off on another one of my outings.

I am trying to formulate a form of words that most properly describes how I am feeling right now, having opened my presents. What fell from the boxes onto my bunk was a cascade of human kindness. The gifts are in themselves simply outstanding, but it is the thoughtfulness that underpinned them that has moved me to a condition of such overwhelming gratitude that I cannot begin to describe it. Gratitude for the simple joy of coming from a loving family, a loving circle of friends and a village community of such benevolent thoughtfulness that I consider myself to have been blessed beyond measure.

To my reader in the Green Man, if you are still sober, please convey my deepest and sincerest thanks to the host of villagers who packed gifts and signed the many cards. You have left me speechless with joy.

The free gift of 600 pints behind the bar, to be supped on my return, was emblematic of so many individual gestures of love that collectively they amount to a tsunami of delight. If that assault of human decency wasn't enough, the "YouTube" clip of my 50th birthday party in the Green Man slaughtered any remnants of composure that I still retained.

The lower lip has wobbled. I confess to having had an unmanly moment. Are you all trying to kill me off with kindness? These presents and the circumstances under which I have received them have made this a profoundly enriching experience. This has come at a good time. I'd spent part of the morning with a man who'd described how he orders bodies to be dumped into villages as evidence of a job well done.

Look not for evil, it is all around me, but for a moment today, it was all swept away. I hope I have expressed myself well enough for you all to know the profound impact you have had on me. As a parting remark, please tell Gary Ives I know full well it was six pints and not 600. However, I needed a response to that shocking close up of him in the YouTube clip and has smile cracking comment about my height.

6th September 2011: If You Can't Beat Them Join Them

Somebody has just toileted my Dutch friend's morale. He has just discovered that had he been a civil servant working out here for NATO, he'd be earning €108,000 per annum, working a 42-hour week and enjoying a month's leave after every three months served.

Moreover, he wouldn't have to carry a gun and shoot somebody if required. I tried to calm him by saying there didn't appear to be an attendant pension, and he responded that on €108,000 tax-free, he would be more than able to make his own provision. How is it, he asks, that his country is planning to sack soldiers on the grounds of affordability when it can afford to fund this largess by the simple expedient of routing it through NATO.

How indeed, thought me. Well, I didn't need to think for much longer because he immediately adopted the adage that if you can't beat them, join them. He promptly completed and submitted his application for said employment, having got me to proof read it first (unwise) and agreeing to act as a referee. This whole scenario reminded me of a comment made by another soldier who likened it out here to a circus.

The lions and tigers were the Taliban, the owners were the contractors making a fortune, and the crowd were the poor soldiers and Afghans who were paying the price. The analogy is perhaps a bit clumsy, but there do appear to be folk making an absolute mint. One sailor I was talking to is starting up an Internet mail-order company for Afghan products like metalwork, rugs and ceramics.

It's all above board. He's found a supplier who will ship the goods to a lock-up somewhere in London from where he will mail out the goods accordingly. He even said he was frontloading the business by covering the Afghan's initial costs. Lots of people make money out of wars, but it's never those who deserve to. He might be the one exception to the rule.

7th September 2011: I Come From Birmingham

He'd wound the window down before the car drew up alongside me. He beckoned me with his left hand to move nearer. I was eight feet distant. His line of fire would have been framed by my body armour. He would have needed me to come closer to get a good shot.

"I come from Birmingham," he added by way of explanation. The driver of the vehicle kept staring to his front. The engine was idling as if he was about to pull away quickly. I could not see the right hand of my interlocutor. It remained firmly hidden behind the door. The pulse quickened. The absence of the normal is the presence of the abnormal.

The scenario did not appear to be one of wanting directions to the Green Man. I was not for budging. This encounter had all the hallmarks of a close-quarter shooting. I'd made my decision I was going to introduce my pistol to the conversation. Then if he did raise a gun to the window, he'd cop it.

The door of the armoured vehicle swung open.

"Get in, we're leaving," the soldier yelled above the noise of the traffic.

My Brummie friend looked surprised. Our blossoming relationship was ended in an instant. I jumped into the back of the vehicle closing the doors behind me. *"He's from Birmingham,"* I told my colleagues. I could see they looked puzzled. The whole exchange had taken less than 5 seconds. I am sure it was nothing. I am sure everything is nothing. But sometimes it's something.

The skill is to figure out when the nothing is something in enough time to keep yourself alive. Our young soldiers go through scenarios like this several times a day. If they haven't recognised the something, they get hurt. If they mistake the nothing for the something they risk prosecution. Quite a baptism for an 18-year-old.

8th September 2011: For General?

"Will it be ready by 1600?" he asked somewhat hopefully as the laundry attendant could barely speak English. *"Four o' clock,"* he added by way of clarification.

The lad remained none the wiser. This verbal jousting was then exchanged for finger gestures, and the lad finally understood.

"No, tomorrow," he said.

"Can I have my laundry back then?" said the American as his bagged knickers were going back and forth like a floor scrubber. As for me, I was beginning to enjoy the spectacle.

"For General?" the Afghan enquired.

"No, mine," came the response. *"But I'm going home early tomorrow,"* the American added.

"Give me the bag," asked the Afghan, and once again, the laundry bounced across the counter. The young lad then whipped out the docket that he had inserted earlier and scrawled across it not "VIP," as I'd seen on a previous occasion, but "EMRG".

Since arriving in Afghanistan, I had certainly seen an emergency into a pair of underpants but never an occasion when the skiddies themselves were the crisis. I know now that if I require my laundry in a hurry, I need only say that it is for the General. In fact, I am minded to do that since Lea's recent parcel included a pair of superman pants.

Indeed, I could go one better and insert some female lingerie. I could then sit back and watch a number of embarrassed Generals trying to quash the rumour that one of them is a closet crossdresser. Well, you've got to keep yourself amused out here somehow.

9th September 2011: Not Aimed at Her

"How the heck do you phone home from the office using paradigm," he demanded. Clearly, something had upset my cellmate, so I enquired as to the source of his angst.

By all accounts, he'd been in one of the telephone booths where soldiers make their paradigm welfare calls home. As I mentioned in an earlier posting, the taxpayer very generously allows each soldier thirty minutes a week of free calls back to Blighty. His call home had been somewhat undermined by a soldier endlessly ranting at his wife for some failure on her part.

He, therefore, wanted to know how he could make such calls from his office. As you know, my affinity for technology is like a Turkey's affinity for Christmas, but I was however able to help. That said, my thoughts turned to the soldier and his wife. It really is not easy being out here. You worry not for yourself but for your family. Simple things like knowing they are going on a long drive play on your mind. I know it sounds silly, but it does.

You feel so helpless totally unable to influence the security of those you love. You find yourself posting messages about what to do and what not to do in an effort to assuage your concerns. I can imagine the source of this soldier's spat. He'd probably asked his wife not to do something. She'd gone and done it and, as a consequence, now had a problem. His rage was perhaps not aimed at her but about his inability and frustration in not being there to help.

Many of the lads are not long wed and have yet to be broken in by their wives and continue, like I once did, to resist the shackles of love. Marriage, though, does seem to be a difficult institution for a frightening number of my colleagues to grapple with. Many of them are either divorced or in the throes of becoming divorced. I make mention of my 21 years (nearly), and they look at me as some kind of ambassador for the cause. Maybe I should set myself up as a marriage counsellor. Or maybe success comes from being naturally good looking with a ready disposition to do the hoovering, washing up, ironing . . .

10th September 2011: Furry Love Cuffs

The Taliban's argument as to their moral superiority over the western world has been somewhat undermined by the activities of one of their numbers with a goat. Sadly for them, our troops are blessed with night vision goggles and other aids of a surveillance nature that makes such proclivities no longer discreet. There is absolutely no privacy here at all, which is why a certain product in the German equivalent of the NAAFI shop had left me puzzled. I hadn't gone in voluntarily, but out of necessity in order to keep track of the bloke who would be driving me. The shop contained the usual Rambo accoutrements such as knives, various weapon holsters and an assortment of other macho merchandise. What did catch my eye, however, were the handcuffs.

Wow, I thought the German military police are a really caring organisation. I say this because they were fur-lined. Indeed, such is the affection for their detainees; they were described as "furry love cuffs". I have either grossly misunderstood their purpose or your average German bobby is an individual blessed of great tenderness towards those he has arrested.

I dismissed the other explanation, which briefly alighted on my neurons, on the grounds of a lack of privacy. It then occurred to me that perhaps in the Teutonic mind, such matters are for public consumption. The German Army has certainly changed since the Wehrmacht, and I, for one, will be keeping clear of the Hun having fun.

This will rule out my participation in their planned alcohol-free Oktoberfest. There are enough things out here to scare the wits out of me, let alone being approached by some lederhosen adorned Saxon clutching a pair of furry love cuffs.

11th September 2011: Two Tablets a Day

To ward off malaria, we take paludrine. The dosage is two tablets a day and four at the start of the week. That makes a total of 16, and they taste vile.

Experience has taught me not to take them on an empty stomach as it brings on a sickness sensation. They come in a blister pack sensibly designed to show you what pills to take on what day. I am sure I have mentioned it before, but the packaging is similar to that found for contraceptive pills.

Even when informed by sensible packaging, concurrent with simple instructions, I still manage to forget to take them. I am not unique in this shortcoming; others report similar challenges. This would explain of course, why when they developed the pill in the 1960s, they did so for the female gender rather than the male. Had they not done so, my experiences out here would suggest that our population would be a lot more substantial than it is today.

Greater Chance of Making It

For the Afghans, childbirth is a traumatic experience, with one in five babies not surviving the process. We, however, are blessed with first-world medical support, which, whilst in no way able to eliminate such heartache, does nevertheless remove it from the national consciousness.

We should be rightly proud of ourselves, but equally, we should not look too harshly on the Afghans for their failure to replicate such high standards. After all, as any informed Afghan may tell you, our rates of abortion are so high that a child conceived in Afghanistan has perhaps a greater chance of making it than one conceived in the UK.

Our values can take a bit of a beating out here, and whilst I am no statistician, I would be interested to know if there is any substance to this perception.

12th September 2011: A Prison of Sorts

"You alright, mate?" I asked as I placed my tray of food down on the table. He looked up and appeared pleased at getting some company. He was a large unit and had been sitting alone. We struck up a conversation. Strap back, I got his life story.

He was a civilian and had been out here for nigh on two years. Although, of course, there were the R&R breaks. He wasn't in one of the best-paid jobs, but a job is a job, a fact which became very apparent in our discourse. An only child, he was a former prison officer who had been made redundant. He spoke with a warm intelligence about those who had been in his custody, which suggested strong suitability for the profession.

The gentleman told me a story of a young man jailed for stabbing a bloke in the street who had been prosecuted for seriously molesting the man's son. The individual died as a consequence of the stabbing. The assailant was subsequently jailed, and every time he goes in front of a parole board, he is asked if he regrets what he has done. He answers that he doesn't, and back to the cells he goes.

Despite being urged to the contrary, the chap says he will not lie. The fate of this prisoner clearly troubled our redundant warden whose parents were also made redundant. For reasons that were unclear to me, they had also lost their home. Being a loving son, he had moved them into his own house and came out here. The chap was very stoical, a characteristic you would expect of a Welshman from the Valleys.

The irony is, like me, he is now in a prison of sorts. This prison however has the added bonus of the possibility of getting shot and there are no visiting rights. We live in two-man cells, eat institutional food, and enjoy the joys of bulk ablutions. One obvious difference between us, however, is that he is out here having been made redundant and I'm out here expecting to be made redundant. We laughed at our situation. I suggested the Army. He looked at me as if I was mad, which I suppose is a self-evident truth; otherwise, I would not be here.

13th September 2011: Crykut

In an effort to improve the physical prowess of this elite formation, of which I am a part, the powers that be have organised a weekly collective physical training session. This can take various forms, and recently it was proposed that the Americans be introduced to cricket. A sport about which I know little and play worse.

As I am not the only Brit this sporting encumbrance was, like my catches, neatly dropped onto the unwilling shoulders of a junior colleague. However, he manfully arranged said event to great effect. Despite coaching, the first American adopted the poise of a baseball player and on striking the ball launched himself horizontally from the stumps before addressing his direction. This was, however, complicated by him having offloaded his bat and retrieving it under the nose of another large yank bearing down on him.

Fortunately, a break down of communication amongst the fielders meant he got away with it. They couldn't bowl so they resorted to what I would describe as a "Botch", a cross between bowling and pitching. Once they got into the swing of things and I mean swing for the bat was moving like a club they seemed to quite enjoy it. Indeed, they enjoyed it enormously, and there was much talk about playing "crykut" again.

This was ironic as you could describe this game in many ways, but cricket wasn't one of them. In fairness though they had excellent hand-eye coordination and would, with training, become quite a force. Before my Green Man reader thinks I've started to swan out here I would add the game lasted a short 60 minutes after which it was back to the grind.

I Think I Want To Go Home

Well, I never. I'd just had a short back and sides when it all starts to kick off. As I go to leave the barbers, I'm swamped as dozens of Afghans start taking cover. It appears we were under attack. While I was deciding how to run away bravely, an Italian in full battle rattle yells out to take cover. I needed no second invitation. Being an old fat knacker, I was ordered to remain undercover while the proper soldiers moved forward to their fire positions.

Two civilians, who clearly thought the war didn't apply to them, decided to chance it. They got about 20 yards when there was the distinctive sound of incoming fire. You should have seen them turn around and leg it back towards where I was standing. I know I shouldn't have, but it was hard not to laugh – the expressions on their faces. As us brave souls hunkered down, some thought it was appropriate to describe the weapon systems.

"That's a suicide vest," says one.

"No, I think it's an RPG," says another.

"I think they are on the other side of the wall," says a Colonel.

"I think I want to go home," says I.

The noise was phenomenal. It sounded like a collective shoot on the ranges. What was starting to bother me was that the firing was intense and sustained, and the explosions appeared awfully close. My mobile goes off.

"Are you alright?" says the Chief of Staff. *"Who is with you?"*

He then asked me to account for our people, so I cut about doing something useful. Remaining in cover at all times, I might add.

A young sailor yells out that an RPG has just flown overhead. At 5' 4" I wasn't bothered. It was the intensity of the machine-gun fire that was troubling me. Just how many are there? It reminded me of that quote from the film Zulu: *"Zulus . . . thousands of 'em."*

Our Afghan interpreter was on the phone. His father, a policeman, had been hurt in the action, but it was only a flesh wound. Blimey, this is serious, and so it was. The fighting went on for hours. The cavalry arrived in the form of an attack helicopter, and you heard the rumble as its cannon opened fire. The enemy had occupied a high building and were bringing their weapon systems to bear. During a lull, people started to filter back outside (not me, I might add). They soon came back in as heavily armed soldiers were posted around us and fed belted ammunition into their machine guns.

"Sir, back inside," came an American accent.

Back inside, I'd no intention of going outside. What was he thinking? It started to rain heavily. Somebody said there was lightning, but it could have been muzzle flashes. I thought it was time to go and get a coffee. I'd actually taken cover in the restaurant. Well, you've got to eat. There I was Mursley's mightiest mariner sipping coffee and watching a replay of the Wales South African game whilst listening to the crump of RPGs and the rat-a-tat of heavy machine gun fire. Wales were robbed.

15th September 2011: Wicked Cause Being Nobly Executed

The battle raged into the night. I found myself holed up with dozens of Afghans, a party from the British Embassy, numerous coalition forces and the Sergeant Major.

By 05:50, I'd been up 24 hours less 20 minutes' broken sleep lying on a tiled floor. Just when you thought it was all over, it would all kick off again. Frankly, I was getting somewhat peeved. It was way past my bedtime, and this unseemly severance from my scratcher was leaving me a bit ratty. By about 10:00 hours, the battle was over. I had, however, gone to the Situational Awareness Centre to watch the final moments unfold. The terrorists were holed up in the steel frame of a hotel that was being constructed. As it lacked outer walls, the CCTV gave a bird's eye view (literally) of the action almost into the heart of the building.

As the last terrorist held out alone against hundreds of troops, attack helicopters and a Special Forces unit moving methodically from room to room, a thought struck me. This was a wicked cause being nobly executed. There is no privacy out here, even in death. Such gallantry did not deserve my gawping at his final moments, so I left.

When the engagement was over, we had to account for all our weapons and personnel. That done, I had some breakfast and then went to the office. By 14:00, I was beginning to wilt, so I had a shave and a shower and took to my bunk. The adrenalin was still pumping, so I returned to the office. Other folk had clearly had a less eventful night as the emails kept coming. I predicted a negligent discharge because people had got a little over-excited. It wasn't long before I was proved correct. The cookhouse is becoming a bullet magnet for all the wrong reasons.

An Extra £10.46

Being a good soldier, I reported into our National Support Element to let my countrymen know I was OK.

While there, I learnt that my extra pay for being out here had been increased from £6.69 per day to £10.46. It is worked out on an increasing scale. The more days you have done on operations, the greater the daily sum. The initial rate is set for the first 340 days, after which it increases as explained. The days are cumulative. We had a similar thing when I was younger, but they changed the model, and I dipped out.

For yesterday's fun and frolics, I was paid an extra £10.46. My German colleague, had he not been on R&R, would have received £95.46 extra. Oh, and for him, it's tax-free. I liked the fact that we both get the same 46 pence due obviously to the current exchange rate. I sometimes wonder who won the war. So does he! By 21:00, I'd given up the ghost and turned in . . . knackered.

16th September 2011: Sliced Boot Garnished With Polish

Queuing for your meals invariably involves lots of banter and a requirement to clear your weapons into the firing bays that are strategically placed in the entrances to what the Americans call a Dining Facility (DFAC).

This is pronounced as "Deefac". To any old soldier reading my posting, a DEFAC would equate to what he or she would understand to be a cookhouse. Such is the quality of the grub; however, outhouse would be a more appropriate noun. It is, however, the clearing of the weapons that has caused great upset amongst High Command rather than the food. We have had a number of negligent discharges as the soldiers have failed to clear their weapons properly. If one is doing so correctly, no harm will be done as the firing bay consists of metal tubes driven into rubble-filled bunkers.

The barrel of your weapon should point down these tubes, which provide the necessary protection should you have got it wrong. Of course, there is the other option, which is simply to discharge your gun straight into the pavement. It seems this is a favoured alternative, albeit unintentionally. Having survived this process, you then have to swipe your card, which allows the contractor to claim the cost of your meal.

In some camps, as a visiting soldier, your card has no validity, so one has to sign a register. There are different registers depending on your nationality, and on entry, the troops sign the appropriate document. However, at one location, they were clearly not used to the British, as we didn't have a register. To my surprise, my colleague suggested signing the one for the French. I objected on the principle of national honour and felt the Jordanian equivalent was the more appropriate on the grounds that their King was the grandson of a British Army Colonel. He then remonstrated with me, claiming that his intent would be the more patriotic. Indeed, he was correct, as it would be the French taxpayer who paid for his meal.

After attributing payment, we are required to wash our hands. This is compulsory, but many have the habit of then blowing their nose into the paper towel they have just dried their hands on, which I thought rather defeats the object of the exercise. No bags (because of the risk of bombs) are allowed in the DFAC and you are also not allowed to wear sunglasses presumably because the eyes would give you away were you to be a suicide bomber.

Of course, this doesn't apply to the Italians, who seem to consider sunglasses a cultural necessity. The hot plate contains a myriad of dishes served up by Indians and Nepalese. The menus are designed to appeal to national tastes but appear to fail as regards British cuisine; less, of course, the curries. The beef and ale pie (minus ale) isn't too bad but the roast beef is a culinary catastrophe resembling sliced boot garnished with polish. The vegetables have been boiled to within an inch of disintegration, which tends to have me favouring the salad.

The food cannot be that bad, I suppose, because we all look healthy enough. And if having a regular constitution is also a sign of good health, then we score well on that account.

17th September 2011: Plenty of Socks

Now that a little time has elapsed, the after-action reports are starting to come in. The winter weather gear that I had applied for, and it seems, had arrived, I will not now be getting.

An RPG had impacted on the container laying waste to its contents. Either that or the QM has come up with a clever wheeze to explain away any shortages. Several lads have asked for a replen of ammunition, which has had High Command asking questions. Our role was not to charge to the ramparts and engage the enemy but let the force protection unit take on that function. Our job was to keep out of their way and, if necessary, remain at our posts. If not, we were to hunker down and provide a reserve.

Well, I have been around long enough to be a little suspicious of this replen request. Ammunition accounting in the Army is a serious business, and any opportunity to make up for a shortfall is perhaps to be welcomed. Claiming to have been involved in a firefight presents an excellent opportunity to do so.

I reflected on my role in the battle and concluded that I had been a good boy. I had not got in the way of those charged with doing the fighting by climbing up on the ramparts with the Macedonians. As if that were likely. No, I hunkered down in the hardened shelter and distributed bottled water to the Afghans who were a little ripe.

Afghan sock has a particular aroma, especially when imbibed with honest sweat. And there was plenty of socks. The toilets were in a state of some distress and at one point I considered the option of simply pointing it round the door as the ablutions began to resemble one giant urinal. The smell would sting your nostrils. Not that these circumstances had anything to do with it but the Sergeant Major and I decided to return to our office. This was sensible as it made us situationally aware and I could brief the rest of the team who were holed up in other parts of the camp. One computer had got shot, but it wasn't mine. The Colonel using it at the time got a bit of a shock, but I'm told these things happen in war.

My Army lawyer friend thought this was all a bit much as she had joked earlier that if she had to deploy with her weapon, then things were seriously amiss. I, however, like "miss" especially when it comes to being shot at. I do not really know if I was ever in any serious danger or indeed how close the bullets actually were because I didn't see the strike marks.

All I heard was the "zing". That said, I did avoid a particularly nasty tripping hazard as I navigated a few steps at speed. I wish somebody had timed me. It could have been a record.

16th September 2011: Garnish With Some Old Cloth

Take two legs of lamb and flash fry for one to two minutes, ensuring that they are brown all over. Meanwhile, boil a pound of rice until it is of a lumpy consistency.

When ready, pour the rice into a white china mixing bowl and then stir in some Marmite until it is dark brown in colour. Having now prepared your lamb and rice, you can take it outside. The best place is pavement with a wall running alongside it. The older and more pitted they are, the better.

Now taking the rice into your right hand, throw it at the wall as if you were creating some modern art. Don't worry if not all of the rice sticks to the wall. This is quite normal, and clumps of the stuff dripping onto the pavement will add to the effect. Having emptied the bowl of its rice, wipe the inside to reveal parts of its creamy white colour.

Place the bowl upside down on the ground and cover it with an old wig. If you don't have a wig to hand, you can use some black wool. Now strike the bowl with a hammer in a short sharp action so as to break it into two or three pieces. Scatter the lamb joints around the bowl in a random fashion.

Garnish with some old cloth. Voila! You have now created the scene of a suicide bomber.

19th September 2011: Answerable to a Higher Authority

Our little Anglican church is steadily growing in numbers. Soon we will be at platoon strength. It is a complete contrast to the vibrant Pentecostal Service where the Preacher plays to a packed house, but it is, in its own way, enormously spiritual and tranquil.

Thus, it is not only the Brits who appear but also the Americans, Kiwis and the occasional European. The Padre is doing a fantastic job, and I have been co-opted to do the occasional reading. Our churchwarden is an intelligence officer. I discovered the other day that he was from the Territorial Army and that in real life, he is a barrister. There is an obvious oxymoron there, but I can't quite pin it down.

However, in his case, that would be an injustice. You only have to sit with him for ten minutes to get a master class in either the law or what is going on out here. No shrinking violet; he has been on several other operational tours. My only criticism is that he was also a Tory district councillor.

As you know my current relations with the Conservatives are less than perfect, and news from home along with their treatment of the military is increasing the

202

divide. That said, with men like him amongst their number, there is hope yet. Not a lot, mind; we can but pray.

Despite my upbeat reports regarding our congregation, there were mutterings in the ranks about the choice of hymns. Last week we had "I vow to thee my Country". This is an extraordinarily powerful hymn, especially for the military. It conjures a myriad of emotions, and for one senior officer, the tears seeped down his cheek.

Making decisions that see men live or die violently can be taxing. For that reason alone, it lifts my heart to see such men in Church. To know that they see themselves as answerable to a higher authority regarding their decisions leaves me feeling comfortable that the boys and girls are in good hands, which is more than you can say for them when I'm hymn singing.

20th September 2011: If Gloating Is a Sin

The Americans are obsessed with PowerPoint as a medium for communication. When I say obsessed, I mean completely and utterly infatuated. We don't have agendas at meetings; we have a PowerPoint slide deck.

Microsoft Word is not the tool of choice for explaining complex scenarios; it all has to go on PowerPoint. I declared my hand very early. I am not a "PowerPoint ranger". Of course, I can throw a few slides together, who can't, but formulating them into what amounts to a storyboard is well beyond my artistic and technical abilities.

This intellectual shortcoming was soon picked up by the General, who viewed my efforts as one would a mishap on the toilet floor. Being a loyal subordinate, I again presented the offending article only to have it described by a colleague as a pile of steaming faeces. This effort, too, did not pass muster, and I had visions of long evening's ahead trying to make a silk purse from a sow's ear.

If gloating is a sin, then I have sinned because my PowerPoint critic was subsequently handed the task. I, of course, remained in the supporting role by offering to fetch a coffee. Credit where credit is due, he produced a good set of slides. However, it still fell to me to write the narrative to go with the brief. Unfortunately, it also fell to me to deliver the brief to a very important person at the daily stand up which is piped into offices throughout the command.

The venue was like something out of a James Bond film with wide screens, imagery, electronic maps and other sophistication, the like of which I could only imagine as a young officer. Indeed, it made the bridge of the USS Enterprise in a modern Star Trek movie look dated. Moreover, my critic, who had described my earlier work so eloquently, threatened to put me off my stride by making faces at me behind the VIP's back.

I took to the floor, lightly touched the lectern, switched on my microphone, took a deep breath and began. I was told afterwards I did really well and sounded like Hugh Grant, until the questions, that is. It appears I reverted to type and was more Bob Hoskins. Despite getting a bit of a verbal beating from a Three-Star General, who had the temerity to disagree with what I'd told the VIP, it was nevertheless, by all accounts, a great honour to have been invited to brief at the "stand up".

The ambitious strive to do so, which begs the question, why me? I struggled for an explanation and then concluded that my film star looks got me the part. I only hope they don't commission a second series. Far too nerve-wracking.

21st September 2011: Billy Big-Stepped

"Did you hear anything about the shooting in Kabul?" phones a Dutchman from Holland.

"Yes, idiot, they were shooting at us," replies my Dutch colleague. And so ended another conversation in the office.

That should have been an end to last week's fun and frolics, but alas, not. Exactly one week later, we were off again. There was a muffled boom, which could be heard across the base. The residence of the former Afghan president had been attacked, resulting in his death. Within seconds the alarms were going off, and the tannoy was blaring away. Like a released spring, I leapt into action, and Billy Big-stepped it to where my body armour was. In seconds I was fully donned in my Robocop kit and hurtling back to my post.

The use of the word hurtling is, in fact, an abuse of the language. All kitted up as I was, I'd only got 50 metres when I was gasping like an asthmatic aardvark. However, there was a strange incentive to keep up the pace, and I must have overtaken several people on route to my combat position. This could also be described as a hidey-hole in a hardened shelter, but combat position sounds more "ally".

We called the roll and then prepared ourselves for a long night. That said, it wasn't long before we were stood down and so ended today's exploits of this lean, mean, green racing machine. Life then continued for us much as normal. I wish I could say the same for a number of lads out in the field and their families.

22nd September 2011: Spread Through Licking

If there are any pussy lovers out there, I would advise you to cease reading. Apart from the Taliban, it now appears that we have rabies to worry about. A directive has been promulgated about the threat of rabies carried by wild animals.

We were ordered to read and sign said directive, which I duly did. On no account are we to touch any animals even if they look harmless. Apparently, there may be no outward signs that the animal is sick, and symptoms can show up sometime after you have been infected.

The animal need not bite you as the disease can be spread through licking. As I have previously reported, our base is inundated with cats, and I fear for their future hence my earlier comment about pussy lovers.

That said, since last week's festivities, they do appear to have thinned out somewhat, or maybe I am just imagining it.

Nasty Niff or Risk a Nasty Nip

Strangely the sign on our accommodation door urging us to keep it shut has been removed and replaced. The original sign required us to keep the door shut so as not to let snakes, scorpions and other nasties into the building.

The new sign now requires us to keep the door open in order to allow fresh air to circulate. I have no idea what is going on here and why there should have been this change. So it's a choice. Spend the night with a nasty niff or risk a nasty nip. The niff must outweigh the nip in terms of nocturnal hazard, so the door stays resolutely open. In the other blocks, the doors are closed. I wonder if somebody is trying to tell me something.

23rd September 2011: Sweet Sticky Phlegm

There are three types of Americans: those who smoke, those who don't, and those who chew tobacco. It is this latter habit which I will now describe. The process involves inserting a plug of tobacco against one's gum under the bottom lip.

This causes intense salivation, which requires the practitioners to regularly vent their spittle. They normally do this into a water bottle or occasionally a coffee cup. This spitting can take various forms: a quick snot effect or a long slow dribble. The accompanying noise is like flatulating into a pair of tight underpants—a bit of a wet squeak which may be prolonged depending on whether you are spitting or dribbling.

Frankly, the habit is utterly disgusting.

It was a long meeting; the PowerPoints were in both English and Dari. I had to concentrate hard. The bloke next to me was chewing tobacco. For three hours, I listened to him spitting and dribbling into his water bottle. I became an authority.

I knew when it was primarily water and when it was mainly phlegm. I glanced across and noticed his water bottle gradually filling with this oily, syrupy dark muck. My water bottle was under my chair; it was hot. We broke for lunch and, on our return, were subjected to another four gruelling hours of death by PowerPoint. Feeling parched, I reached under the chair for my water bottle but alas I had mistaken my original seat. Concentrating on the slide being presented, I unconsciously undid the lid and took a deep swig to quench my thirst. The assault on my senses was ruthless.

The sweet sticky phlegm induced consistency saturated my taste buds in an orgy of horror. My English reserve was parked abruptly as this foul slurry was projected from my mouth. The General was lucky not to take it down his back. The Sergeant Major chased after me with a bottle of freshwater as I took off for the door. To my reader in the Green Man, I apologise for putting you off your pint. This was by far the worse experience of my tour thus far. It was far worse than being under fire and demonstrably more unpleasant than giving blood.

Every American in my unit is now fully aware of my thoughts regarding chewing tobacco. Enjoy your dinner. I haven't since.

24th September 2011: To Whom It May Concern

I'm not sure who it is, but I need to thank somebody. I'd left my superman underpants (courtesy of Lea) in the shower block, and some kind soul had ensured I got them back.

It must have involved some degree of handling, which couldn't have been pleasant. Such consideration has not been extended to the soldier who has put up a poster asking for the return of his body armour and helmet. An individual has misappropriated them, which frankly is a diabolical thing to do in a war zone. Although after recent events I can understand why they have become such attractive items.

I nearly reacquainted myself with my battle rattle this morning as I could hear gunfire. However, we were "tannoyed" that this gunfire was in honour of a former President whose funeral it was. It was hardly a volley, more like spraying of bullets. It is all very well sending these bullets up but what I want to know is where are they all going to land.

It's not the bullet with my name on it, which bothers me so much, but rather the one with "to whom it may concern".

25th September 2011: The Afghans Are Too Polite

I felt lost, sat as I was, in the Minister for what not's office. My pen was poised as my notebook rested precariously on my knee. 'Blow that for a game of soldiers', I thought as I dragged a coffee table a little closer and reassigned my scribing efforts from my knee to the table.

A servant brought out a tray of tea, the colour of which was light yellow which resembled a well-known waste product. It tasted much like those trendy teas such as Earl Gray, which are fashionable in England. I thought about asking for some milk but restrained myself. The waiter also brought out trays of nuts and sweets. I thanked him in Dari, but I don't think my command of the language impressed him too much.

I declined to avail myself of this generosity, as I did not want to embarrass myself wrestling with a pistachio nut whilst taking notes. The meetings start off with polite introductions as to the well being of one's family. This is a pooh trap for the unwary as you do not ask an Afghan about female or elderly relatives. As I was in the supporting role, I was not involved in this stage of the proceedings, which was just as well. It would have been inappropriate to comment on my girls, and my having four brothers and over a dozen nephews would likely push the meeting into the following day.

Taking minutes is, however, made easy because everything is translated from Dari to English and English to Dari. This gives you a chance to catch up. However, for that advantage, there is, of course, a disadvantage, which is that the interpreter will have an accent and may not be able to translate succinctly into English what was said in Dari. I do not minute all that is said. This is not because of disparaging comments. The Afghans are too polite, but rather because I feel some remarks are too candid and therefore a little dangerous.

Once I gather all this information, I fashion it into documents that are then used to inform national policy.

It is strange to think that I joined the Army to be a rufty tufty soldier. I had no idea that one day they would ask me to assume the role of a secretary. Frankly, I don't have the legs for it (unlike Trent Baker). That said, they should send me to work for Dominique Strauss Kahn. With his antics, he'd get a lot more than he bargained for.

26th September 2011: No Good Deed Goes Unpunished

My loathing for the European Union has today reached stratospheric levels. As a soldier, I had thought I was immune from this temple of incompetence, but no. Sadly, this institution of ineptitude has clobbered me right on the back of the head.

Why, I ask myself? I am not a businessman struggling with more EU layers of bureaucracy. I'd already accepted that the thumb sucking intellects who masquerade as our politicians would never do anything to upset their new master.

Indeed, I'd even come to terms with the Coalition sacking soldiers and closing care homes whilst increasing our annual tribute. No, dear reader, the source of this spluttering of spittle is that they have robbed me of my wingman. One of my Flying Dutchman's job applications has proved successful. Working as he was under the threat of redundancy, who can blame him for taking matters into his own hands?. He had the telephone interview yesterday, and today the EU offered him a job. Clearly not as bankrupt as it'd have you believe. His future in Afghanistan is set to improve dramatically with three months leave a year, a considerably enhanced salary and his own private en-suite accommodation. I blame myself; after all, I helped him with his application.

As they say, no good deed goes unpunished. That said I'm happy for him. He may well have secured his future, and the EU trough runs deep. The Sergeant Major and I are about to become much busier.

27th September 2011: More Billy Biscuit

Like every British soldier, I have been trained to kill. The prospect of having to do so is decidedly unwelcome, but years ago, I accepted it as a condition of employment.

That being the case, one would think I'd a hardened approach to life and its misfortunes. Well, I haven't, and my attitude to the children who accost me when I leave the base has changed completely. Yes, I know I shouldn't, but I cannot help myself. I give them sweets.

I can no longer bear the expectant look of disappointment as I, like hundreds of others, shoo them away. They are noble-looking youngsters with a quick smile and chirpy demeanour. They have squat in life, and yet I have abundance in all thing's material and spiritual.

Had I been born here, with my start in life, I'd be one of them. So, there you have it I'm a big softie. Well, all right, a little softie. As I part with sweets, I imagine that it is the children in my village handing them out.

This is from Lucy. This is from Mia. Sam and Josh have given you this and so on. Little Archie, who I have yet to meet, has been quite generous in his turn. Even the poor cripple in the cart has copped some goodies. I know I shouldn't, and perhaps somebody will have words, but up with this, I can no longer put. There I confess all. More Billy Biscuit than Willy Wonka, but I am what I am.

28th September 2011: Bald, Pitted and Torn

With my rifle slung across my chest, I strode purposefully up the hill, my battle rattle weighing heavily on my shoulders. There was an articulated lorry parked on the side of the road facing down the slope. Under each of the wheels, the driver had placed a rock.

As I walked past, I noticed the condition of the tyres. They were bald, pitted and worn. Chunks of rubber had been ripped from the tread, and I wondered how on earth it had survived the mountain passes. All in all a shabby looking vehicle despite the bright colours and attendant artwork. That said, the driver's confidence in his rig clearly surpassed mine by a huge margin.

The evidence for that assertion is that on looking under the truck, I saw that he had laid out a rug and was dozing in the heat of the day with a sheet over him. Well, I never. What with the rocks under the wheels, suggesting dodgy brakes, and being on a slope, I did wonder if there wasn't a chance that the truck would get underway of its own accord. Were that to happen, our Afghan trucker might find his afternoon siesta taking on an air of permanency. Having said that, he had clearly done some sort of risk assessment as he'd positioned himself midway between the wheels. Presumably, were the worse to happen, the truck would glide effortlessly over him, leaving him safe in his slumbers.

As I stared at him, he glanced up at me and was probably more worried about being gawped at by a heavily armed British soldier than any threat his truck might present. I said cheerio and moved on.

29th September 2011: Crashed and Burned

Bad news for the flying Dutchman. His ambition to snout in the EU trough has come to nought. It appears the Dutch Navy is still minded to make him redundant on their terms and was not prepared to release him early.

The flying Dutchman's ambitions have therefore crashed and burned. As his superior, I felt the need to offer some counselling but "suck it up cupcake" was perhaps the wrong approach. He's to be married for the first time next spring, and I'm impressed that he has held out so long. We have worked up a plan B.

He is more cheerful now, especially as he has secured an interview with NATO as a civilian. Being in the military is a little like prison; you cannot leave just when you want to. The timings for this NATO job are a little more plausible. I'm overhearing a lot of Dutch at the moment, but I don't think it is suitable for polite company.

Stag on

It must be my broad shoulders, but another officer was sharing his woes with me yesterday. His replacement has been suspended over an issue in Iraq, which is currently topical in the media.

He has been told to stag on for another three months. This will be a difficult conversation with his wife. As he's a paratrooper, I restrained myself from the "suck it up cupcake" approach for fear of being thrown over the balcony. "Oh dear, how sad, never mind," wasn't much better either.

Various Injuries

Another officer, however, is being sent home for an operation. He'd sat for two hours crossed-legged at a shura (meeting) and got up a bit too sharpish. This resulted in various injuries to the knee. He may well have been sitting with his battle rattle on, so that would have been quite a weight if he'd got up awkwardly.

There's a rumour that my successor has taken up free-fall parachuting and full contact rugby. He'd better not. If he injures himself and I end up staying on for another three months, there will be trouble.

30th September 2011: Slip It on Like a Shirt

Top tip when wearing body armour. Slip it on like a shirt rather than pulling it over your head like a jumper. That way, you won't crack your skull open on the metal plates.

Make sure you haven't left anything in your shirt pockets because you will not be able to access them with any ease. Moreover, the weight of the armour will press the contents into your chest, which will leave you decidedly uncomfortable. There is also the potential for embarrassment as you walk down the road with your mobile chirping away.

This rather ruins the macho image. The body armour has Velcro fastenings, which are enormously effective. So much so that when dressing in your cell, you can, if you are not careful, leave the room with a bathroom towel and other accoutrements in tow. The outside of the body armour is covered with elasticated strips, which allow you to attach pouches and a holster. The temptation is to slot other useful items into the elastic, but we are told not to do this. In an explosion, they will become detached and cause a further fragmentation hazard.

If it happens to be a bayonet inserted between these elasticated strips, then you will create real problems. I tend

224

to keep my bayonet under lock and key for fear of inadvertently stabbing myself. It's been a while since I've been on the bayonet range. If I remember correctly, I used to quite enjoy the experience, charging across a field and then thrusting it into a series of dummies whilst yelling like a banshee.

Nowadays, I'd probably trip over my bootlaces. The purloined body armour that I reported on earlier has still not been returned. I thought about putting a label in mine, but with my unique sizing qualities, it is unlikely to be nicked.

October 2011: Redundant Soldier

Can you see away a head?
With a P45 and a mate that's dead?
You joined a family, or so you thought,
But the bankers' greed has left you caught.

Caught for want of a mortgage payment,
Caught for want of a plus bank statement.

The Treasury sacked you, and now you're poor,
The wife has left you, and you're out the door.

Is this the lot of a redundant soldier,
Finding a doorway before it's colder?

Cameron's warm at the dispatch box,
The green bench polished by the arse of Fox.
Rough sleepers not wanted in Parliament Square,
Your mate's alright; he died out there.

1st October 2011: More Windmill than Wigwam

All change at the sharp end. I have a new boss the American has gone only to be replaced by a Dutch General. Moreover, he has brought with him a plethora of Dutchman as well. The culture in the branch is about to change from being US-centric to Dutch.

More windmill than wigwam. Clearly, the accents are different, and occasionally they revert to the hurdy-gurdy. The Flying Dutchman is delighted at having so many of his countrymen around. My Dutch history is limited to William of Orange, the battle of Sole Bay and some altercation with the Spanish. As for the culture, I think I'm up with the hunt.

Tulips, polders that sort of thing. My German colleague was looking a bit pensive (they invaded Holland in three days), but his portfolio has followed the outgoing American. To bring further joy to the Flying Dutchman, he's off on leave in the next few days. It's proving difficult to make him unhappy at the moment, but I'm sure I'll think of something.

A British Army Officer has just got away, which was a source of much relief to us. He needed to get home as his daughter is scheduled for some major surgery, which was an obvious worry to him. Before he left, he complained of an earache and went to see the quack. She referred him to a specialist to rule out cancer. What a thing to be told in a place like this what with his daughter an' all.

His family has gone to the top of my prayer list.

Afternote: The British Army Officer did, after all, have cancer. A brain tumour was removed.

2nd October 2011: Church Warden

Prior to my departing Blighty, a well-loved friend called Andrew Cowell remarked at the lengths people will go to get out of being the churchwarden. This was a slanderous accusation, but I was nevertheless amused by it. That said, the Lord moves in mysterious ways.

Apparently, my regular church attendance here on base has not gone unnoticed. I was sounded out accordingly by the current churchwarden, who felt I was the ideal man to step into the breach. A copy of the Church Times on my desk may have cemented this perspective.

While it is a good read, it may just have dropped me in it. Although the prospect of perhaps being the first Mursleyite to assume such a position in Afghanistan did have a certain charm, I was nevertheless reticent. Not for reasons of idleness but simply because a young infantry Major that I know has recently arrived. He is a very spiritual man and has applied to become a Church of England curate.

I cannot pretend to understand the process, but an initial interview seems to have gone well. Therefore, I have selflessly stepped aside and given him an excellent recommendation for the appointment. The post of the churchwarden, I am sure, will support him in his second career. Seems odd, though, that a man whose skill is to arrange meetings between people and their maker should now want to prepare them for the event instead.

Maybe it's not so odd after all. I cannot think of one who would be better placed, in fact.

3rd October 2011: 20' by 8'

Being a former sea captain, I undertook a number of voyages delivering ISO containers to Belgium. It seems ironic that I should now live in one. In fact, the modern military has taken to these boxes like it once did for tents.

Both my living quarters and office space are made up of containers. To make a building, the containers are simply bolted together, having been fitted out with a door and window. The larger the building, the more containers there are. You can create two storeys.

It's all rather like a giant Lego set. The accommodation for the two of us is a single container measuring 20' by 8'. Each of us, therefore, has 10' by 8 feet of living space.

Get Out and Stay Out

I discovered this morning that Hell hath no fury like a Frenchman kept awake by a dodgy fire alarm. He'd obviously had a disturbed night (unlike me!) and had had about enough of it. Within minutes of his call, the fire department was in attendance. I'm always a bit nervous about folk playing around with fire alarms in case they knacker them. Our sleeping area is full of small arms ammunition, and a fire would be decidedly unwelcome and require our immediate departure.

Doing so as ammunition cooks off would certainly put a spring in my step. As a gesture to fire safety, I sometimes wear a wristband, which advises that in the event of a fire, one should "Get out and stay out". Some wag thought it was a protest against being in the Army.

Make the Best of It

The office which I share, with three others, is also a container. These containers are known as "Corimecs" which is a corruption of a brand name that is applied to all such structures regardless of manufacturer.

If I were a General, I would have two containers for my office, but I'm not, so the three of us make the best of it. They are warm and dry, and the metal walls allow us to use magnets to hang maps and diagrams. The Dutchman and I have pictures of our respective sovereigns, which are a bit of a mystery to the American Sergeant Major. I also have a picture of Yvonne Fletcher, in honour of her memory, and in the hope that now we are in Libya, we will get the murderer responsible for her death.

Not that Yvonne will get justice however. Nowadays you only get a legal process.

4th October 2011: Working His Bouffant

As I strolled towards the ablutions for my morning constitution, I was taken aback by the unmistakable sound of a hairdryer. I naturally assumed it must be an RAF officer, but it was a little too early for that.

I solved the mystery when I saw a bloke working his bouffant with a dryer and hairbrush. To my alarm, he was, in fact, a soldier. To my relief, he wasn't one of ours . . . he was a German. Clearly, in my follically challenged circumstance, I would have no need for such a device.

That said, in all my 27 years in the Army, this is the first time I've seen a soldier on operations, or exercise, with a hairdryer. I think even our girls would blush at the prospect. Of course, I cannot speak for the RAF.

Laughing Dutchman

One has to accept that folk from overseas may have a different outlook on life, and this blend of many nationalities does make life exceedingly interesting. I have a small section, which is part of a larger team. I have mentioned the Flying Dutchman on several occasions.

Like most of his kind, he stands well over six feet tall. He's always laughing, which cheers me enormously. Perhaps I should describe him as the "Laughing Dutchman". He seems to have spent years in harm's way in some hellhole trying to stop genocide of one form or another. I sometimes wonder, after what he has been through, how he still has the capacity to laugh.

The Sergeant Major

Then there is the Sergeant Major. It is rumoured that he is the consequence of a love affair between an African American and a German girl when his Dad returned from Vietnam. This curtails my German jokes somewhat, but I am extraordinarily fond of him. He works hard and loves his wife and their five children. You can get to know a man really well through sharing an office when he rings home. He always carries his bible with him, in which he has highlighted his favourite pieces of scripture.

An Amazingly Talented and Gifted Bunch of People

It must be my magnetism, but the boss has given us another Dutchman who appears to like fishing. Moving out of our section, we have the wider branch. Naturally, there are many Americans for whom this is yet another war.

It's the poverty in their own country that keeps them mindful about money being spent here. A surprising number of them are pilots, as is the El Salvadorian whose profession is to land tough men in difficult places. Then we have the doctors. One of whom asks me to check his draft staff papers. It seems that when it comes to paperwork, doctors are the same the world over.

What he gives me is the equivalent of a 20-page prescription. Needless to say, it takes me a while to sort it out. Our German paratrooper seems to like my jokes which is just as well as I hold nothing back. Occasionally, he has a cause to go into the Polish General's office, which has me chasing after him. When he asks me what I want, I tell him I'm there to make sure he doesn't occupy the place. I'm helping a Pole source a pair of British Army boots. As he is a sailor and not a soldier, I assume he doesn't know much about boots.

Also, in the corridor is an American Admiral who frequents both the Church and the gym on a Sunday. We have a Malaysian who is really easy to get on with. He's a Muslim who is surrounded by the occasional Bible and Christian icon, and on a Friday morning, he's off to the mosque.

The Belgian and our two Czechs have returned home to be replaced by more Dutchmen. I liked the Belgian and the Czechs too. To be absolutely frank, as a group, they are an amazingly talented and gifted bunch of people. Even some of the Americans speak a couple of languages. The International coalition, perhaps with one notable exception (i.e. me), must have sent their very best here. I count myself privileged to be included amongst their number.

Somebody joked that while things were difficult, we were not trying to solve world hunger. The irony is that if you took out the politics, this lot could do just that.

5th October 2011: The Spellchecker is English (UK)

I know I have given earlier insights into the language challenges of working out here, but I thought my reader in the Green Man would want me to expound a little. Apparently, somebody had "verbalised" an issue to a colleague. This, in plain English, means he told him about it.

Then there is the primary, alternate, contingency and emergency or PACE plan. This is what you and I would know as a backup plan, or in British Army speak, a contingency plan. Being asked to comment on "command and control and structural authorisations and fills" had me floundering in desperation.

Sometimes I reassure the Americans that when I am not tracking an issue, I am perhaps following it. Then there is the spelling. Apparently, one Aussie went through an entire order changing "ize" to "ise" as in organise.

Being a good soldier, I have checked the relevant NATO Standing Operating Procedure (SOP), and it makes it quite clear that the default setting for the spellchecker is English (UK).

It then came as a bit of a surprise to see another SOP talk about "organization and processes". The words "programme", "centre" and "colour" are firm favourites for confusion as indeed is "favorites" itself.

Having said all of that, I'm not too hot at spelling myself, so I'm sure that most of it doesn't pass me by. The yanks like to synchronize while I like to coordinate. Then there is "socialize". I'd assumed we were off to a party when in fact, to socialize a document is to let other people see it before publication.

But if ever you find yourself in an ongoing standby situation, you might want to simply state that you are waiting. I could write for hours on this subject, but instead, I'll verbalise (sorry verbalize) you all about it when I get home. Meanwhile, I must go and get an azimuth check from the General . . . whatever that might be?

6th October 2011: Proud of My Profession

Word had reached my nautical ear that my successor had been selected for redundancy. This begged the obvious question as to who would relieve me. I made a desperate call to the Army Personnel Centre, fearing that they might have some bad news in the form of "suck it up cupcake".

Without an employment contract or a trade union to defend my interests, a simple stroke of the pen would mean, by law, I'd have to remain in place. This was not an enchanting prospect, and I'm not much cop at digging tunnels.

It came as a huge relief to learn that when one is a volunteer for redundancy, he or she is still required to do their assignment. I will therefore be replaced as planned. Flap over, or as our illustrious Prime Minister said: "Calm down, dear". Still, it does beg the question as to how motivated my successor will be. I suspect he will be highly motivated, which makes me proud of my profession.

More Money for the EU Tribute

Incidentally, earlier in the week, a chap told me his wife had been made redundant from the military. This came as a shock, as he would have liked to have been at home to offer her support. It is a shame that they sacked her within two years of her receiving an immediate pension. That'll be a big saving for the Chancellor mind. More money for the EU tribute. Well, those MEPs earn their money, and it does explain how they can afford mistresses.

7th October 2011: How Sweet

I hesitated and felt socially awkward. The Afghan female was reaching across to shake my hand. We were in the office of somebody important, and I didn't want to make a Horlicks of things. We had been briefed that we were not to touch females and the etiquette if introduced, was to simply place your hand over your heart.

The girl was quite purposeful in her body language, so I no longer recoiled and shook her hand. Of course, back in Kensington, there would have been air kisses and "hello darlings", but out here, this would be entirely inappropriate. The Afghan males will, however, embrace and kiss each other on the cheek. This is a far more deliberate affair than, say, in France.

Males holding hands are entirely normal. One of our civilian advisors (a former paratrooper and Vietnam veteran) did his duty and, for 90 minutes, walked round a bazaar holding an Afghan General's hand. Unfortunately for him, this did not go unnoticed, and photographs have been circulated. What made it the more uncomfortable for this old soldier was that they were wearing matching jackets . . . how sweet.

I was surprised at the Afghan female being so forward, but then the situation became clear. She was an Afghan American and, along with her "business partner", had returned to Afghanistan to help get the country back on its feet. He was an interesting character, having deserted the Afghan Army when it operated under Soviet direction.

In fact, he'd deserted twice, and his family found $4000 so that he could flee to the USA. The American dream lived up to expectations, and here he was, a successful entrepreneur back in Afghanistan. I asked if he intended to remain here or return to America.

He said the former, but I am not so sure. Not that I'm implying anything, but there seems to be an abundance of opportunities to make money if you know, or are of, the culture. I'm sure the temptation to milk it for all its worth and send the money out of the country would prove quite a temptation.

Not that it applies in this case, of course. Only the office in which we had gathered belonged to a gentleman who said things that made me feel decidedly uncomfortable. And I'm not talking about the impending England v France game.

8th October 2011: Not Bloody Likely

"Where are you off to, lads?" I enquired while walking across the base.

"We're off to play touch rugby. Why don't you come along, sir?" came the resply.

I pondered this generosity for a moment and then stupidly said yes. The pitch resembled the film set of "Tobruk". It was a combination of sand and sparse grass with the odd patch of concrete. As if that wasn't bad enough, there was a path made up of stones, which ran along the edge of what passed for a try line.

I thought about arranging an urgent call on my mobile but in all conscience, I couldn't. The lads were supposed to be playing with the Afghans, but the team was in Pakistan on a seven's tournament. We, therefore, played amongst ourselves. When we say ourselves, I would include the Americans and the French. It was hot, dusty and hard work. Being touch rugby, I naively expected it would be just that . . . touch.

No such luck. I must have been bounced more often than the ball. My mind was writing cheques that my body couldn't cash. Knowing that "speedy" is not my middle name, I would try and receive the ball at pace to compensate for lack of acceleration. This would make the "collisions" all the more painful. I suffered for over an hour until it got dark, which came as a blessed relief.

"See you again next week," says a chirpy jock Corporal. Not bloody likely, thought I.

9th October 2011: I Don't Want a Job

"Hello, Englishman, give me five pounds, please."

"No."

"Give me 50 pounds, please."

"Look, why would I have English money when I'm in Afghanistan?"

"Then please give me Afghan money."

"Why would I have Afghan money when I'm an Englishman?"

The lad then looked puzzled. He must have been about 13.

"Anyhow, why are you not at school?"

"I don't want to go to school."

"Then how will you get an education and a job?"

"I don't want a job."

"Then how will you get money?"

"You will give it to us."

"No, we will not."

He looked a little crestfallen, so I discreetly slipped him and his little friend a sweet to cheer them up.

He popped it in his mouth and then screwed up his face in disgust.

"Take the wrapper off, son; it will taste better."

With that, he smiled, stopped in the street and said goodbye.

His English is good, and he is a tough-looking lad. He'll keep learning English from the soldiers, and then one day perhaps he will be an interpreter for a British Infantry Regiment.

I suspect he's fond of the British. He'd approached me and not the American. Who knows the casual gift of a sweet may one day see him save the life of a soldier. It has happened. Young children putting their lives on the line to warn our lads of danger. What price a sweet? Still, he was a stroppy mite. Well, that's teenagers for you.

10th October 2011: Four Kilos Lighter

He sat there smiling as she stretched out across his lap. As he stroked her shoulders, she arched her back and purred softly.

"What the heck are you doing with that cat?" I enquired. *"You'll likely catch rabies. Haven't you read the warnings."*?

"Relax," came the reply. *"This cat has been neutered and vaccinated. Look at its collar."*

True to his word, the cat did indeed have a collar and a name, too. My original concern for the camp's moggies reported in an earlier post was obviously unfounded. It seems that this particular fighting force is a bunch of pussie lovers. This is because the Base Commander had organised a visit by some veterinarians who had rounded up all the cats.

Once they were captured, the vets had them neutered and vaccinated. To complete this process, a collar with a name badge was placed around the neck. The cats, like us, are required to display their name badges at all times when on the base.

Cats without name badges are to be reported to the Base Commander. Quite how one is to do this is a mystery to me. Unlike the cats' badges, our name badges can give the onlooker a rough idea as to how long we have been in Theatre. This is because they include a photograph that was taken when we arrived. If you resemble your picture, you haven't been here for very long. If, however, you look drawn by comparison, then that indicates you have been around for a while.

I'm now in the latter category being some four kilos lighter than when I arrived.

11th October 2011: Storm Related Noise

It was one heck of a bang. I knew it was loud because it woke me up. The last time an explosion roused me was when the oil storage tanks in Hemel Hempstead blew up.

It must have been the mountains, which magnified the noise. Almost immediately, I heard the alarms going off, albeit they were distant. However, there was something distinctly familiar about this particular "boom" so I rolled over and went back to sleep.

The colleague who was reported to have run down the corridor half-naked clutching an assault rifle obviously thought differently. Although it took me a few moments to collect my thoughts, I knew exactly what that noise was. It was a weather phenomenon known as thunder and lightning. In truth, though, I'd never heard such a storm-related noise quite like that before. The intensity was somewhat alarming . . . well, for a moment anyway.

Clearly, though, I am not that tuned into natural events because an earth tremor was reported a few weeks ago, which had no effect on my slumbers. The US Marine insisted he'd been woken by an earthquake. I think he was imagining it; more like something he'd eaten.

12th October 2011: Pork Is in Abundance

He stopped and looked longingly at the offering. I looked too but had no idea what it was. It resembled cheese on toast with globules of meat dribbled into it. The chap continued to hesitate. He then looked down at me (he was a big lad) . . . : *"Pork?"*

Well, it comes to something when you find yourself the principal catering adviser to a large Turkish Muslim who can't make his mind up about a dish. Well, I had absolutely no idea I could barely make out the cheese.

"Hang on."

And with that, I scooped up a lump of the substance with my fork.

"It's beef," I announced with a barely disguised air of culinary sophistication. The big lad smiled and heaped a couple of portions onto his plate.

I think we could be a little more accommodating of our Muslim soldiers. On the hot plate, pork is in abundance. It comes in all sorts of disguises, but I can nevertheless spot it.

I suppose it is a cheap cut compared with beef or lamb. The bacon resembles something put through a mangle and deep-fried. I think it is in the American style. The point about the pork is that there is too much of it, and I feel sorry for the Muslim folk. Imagine having to face every day a hot plate groaning with cooked dog. We wouldn't like it at all.

I apologise to my reader in the Green Man if he has just invested in a pig farm, but you get my point? The Korean soldiers on the other hand . . .

13th October 2011: Rain

As I type this latest posting, my right ear is half-cocked, listening in to the daily brief, which is piped through our computers. The briefing officer is currently describing the manner in which some poor soldiers have died. Earlier, we had the meteorologist give the weather forecast.

This is useful stuff for our pilots, and it is always a comfort for a soldier to know whether he's to be soaked in a downpour or baked to a frazzle, or both. He can then set himself up for the day, having decided in advance what to whinge about as a means of improving morale.

There does appear to have been a shift in the weather with the onset of October. I have been rained on, and the temperature has dropped markedly. Currently, it's rather like a wet August bank holiday when you ask yourself why you didn't go abroad for your vacation.

I much favour this liquid sunshine over the scorching heat, although colleagues from warmer climes would disagree. Some folk are walking about in Gortex jackets, but as one Royal Marine remarked, we are not exposed to the elements for long enough to need them. Besides, as the weather can be close, they make you sweat something horrible. Long may this spell of English weather continue.

Stand fast Salisbury Plain Training Area, but I really do not mind the rain. The meteorologist has told us we are in for snow this winter. Three feet in some parts. No doubt the airport will get snowed in just as I'm scheduled to fly home. It rained during the bomb scare, which didn't please the lads manning the cordon. But to be frank, rain is the least of our worries.

14th October 2011: Armalites for Aid

When I was a little lad, one of my earliest memories was sitting down in front of a black and white TV watching a news report showing an African boy starving. Even as an infant, I figured that that was bang out of order, and surely it would get sorted. Decades later, I once again found myself sat down in front of a TV, albeit colour, watching a news report showing an African boy starving.

These recollections triggered by I know not what gave me the belief that my generation was pretty hopeless. Our parents and grandparents destroyed Nazism and Japanese imperialism, and we can't even put a plate of grub in front of a wee lad.

The reason why this would be occurred to me when I was in the Balkans and in Iraq. You can do all the good in the world, but it amounts to nothing if those for whom you do it are not secure. A similar problem exists out here. The prospect of starvation is a real issue. Fifty per cent of the calories consumed comes from wheat, and yet the seed quality is poor, and crop disease is rife.

In other words, the Afghan farmers need some help and advice. The trouble is your average agricultural subject matter expert cannot exactly bimble up to Waheed's wheat farm because the baddies may well come over the hill and make life pretty unpleasant. This is where American ingenuity comes in. What they have done is identified their farm boys who are serving in the US Reserves and configured them into self-contained volunteer units.

These units are then sent out into the field to help Waheed and his ilk. When the baddies come over the hill, they then discover a group of Nebraskan stalk chewers and the business end of their assault rifles. They are an armed aid agency. Were they to be unarmed, they'd be a dead aid agency, and Waheed would go without. I think this approach has merit. Help those who need it and harm those who try and stop you. Maybe the world needs a new charity that, instead of harmlessly helping and having to thin out when the going gets tough, they could be aggressively ameliorating.

I've even thought of a name for it. "Armalites for Aid" or "A4A".

15th October 2011: Bob Hope and No Hope

There was talk of sending me into the mountains. Not these mountains, however, but the ones in Norway. It was all shaping up to be a rather jolly event with a two-week pass out of Afghanistan.

The suggestion was that I go to the Joint Warfare Centre at Stavanger and help train the next tranche of staff officers. For some reason, I thought this was an extremely good idea. Norway in December would be quite delightful, and I'm sure I could cope with the shock of expensive beer. It was all looking good. After all, they'd given me the problem of working up some training requirements and help develop the attendant lesson plans.

Oh yes, this modern version of the great escape was shaping up nicely. I could just see myself off duty sitting in a Scandinavian hot tub admiring a seafood menu and debating whether to go for a barrel-fermented Chardonnay or perhaps a Chablis. Or why not both? This would surely be the view of my reader in the Green Man. To coin an army expression, it seems I had two hopes "Bob Hope" and "no hope." The Deputy Commander of our little huddle of hardened troops called me into his office. He told me I wasn't going now; I couldn't be spared.

One of the Dutchmen who'd been in Theatre less time than a dogwatch would be going instead. I tried to convince him I could speak Norwegian I even threatened to start crying. It was all to no avail. Crisp winter evening strolls along the seashore would be the preserve of a Dutch colleague. I wonder if I could persuade him to play rugby. Well, you know how easy it is to break a leg . . .

16th October 2011: X-Factor Royalty

I know I have a great face for radio, but I didn't think the Army would pick up on it. However, they have, and I am now in receipt of orders as to my next assignment. I'm delighted to report that I will be returning to England, and although this may have an adverse impact on house prices, I am nevertheless pleased.

As to my next appointment, it involves media operations . . . whatever that might be. I know it will involve quite a bit of training, but as to the details, I am not quite sure. I will, of course, be knocking around with some media types and who knows the odd celebrity or two.

Indeed, while she didn't make a point of coming to see me, the luscious Cheryl Cole did take time out to visit some of the lads in Theatre. This was a huge morale boost for the boys.

A colleague who later visited their location was happy to learn that he had been allocated the very same room that this X Factor royalty had stayed in. Although perhaps disappointed at the sequencing, he was however delighted at the prospect of sleeping in the very same bed.

That said, all was not well on the night. Despite the room being cosy with a wafting ambience of expensive perfume, all was indeed not well. The lads had stripped it bare. There wasn't a sheet, pillow, slip, or duvet to be had. They'd taken the lot. It brings a smile to my face to imagine these young heroes wrapping themselves up at night in Cheryl's former bed linen in what will be the cold plains of Afghanistan. Then, of course, it could all be on eBay!

17th October 2011: We Do It Well

Death and injury are briefed as if they were traffic reports. This may seem callous, but it is the nature of the business. It comes with turf. When it rains, you get wet, and when there's a war, you get death and injury.

At the strategic level, death is reported in a very matter of fact way. Notwithstanding this, any loss is treated with huge reverence by the Commands. The troops will parade when the departed are carried aboard the aircraft. This is known as a ramp ceremony. The military is very good at this. We do it well. We know how to honour people. Whilst all of us want to avoid being listed on the local war memorial, you have to accept that it may happen. It is an old cliché, but out here, life is cheap, and that includes your own.

It doesn't just apply to Johnny Foreigner in his flip-flops and unusual headgear. It applies to us all. Our lives are no more important than theirs. I'm not sure all of us out here would accept that, but that is how I see it. Death can be sudden and unexpected. For our fighting soldiers, it is an ever-present reality as they daily commit to operations. For the old fat knackers in the rear, it is at a much greater distance. A negligent discharge and being shot by a renegade Afghan have carried two souls off that I'm aware of.

This is quite apart from the deaths, which occurred during what is known irreverently as the Battle of Taliban Tuesday. The after-action reports are quite graphic. Bullets don't leave holes; they slice you up. Having a soldier describe what it's like to cut a man in half with a machine gun can put you off your lunch. I cannot begin to imagine what it is like to have actually done it.

18th October 2011: Suckers for Punishment

He glanced up at the photographs of my family on the office wall. The Afghan interpreter was clearly inquisitive, so I explained that I had two daughters. He liked the pictures but said that in his country, he would not have images of females on public display. I asked him if he had any children. My use of the word "children" rather than "daughters" was deliberate in order not to cause any offence. Notwithstanding my diplomacy, he did explain that he had a baby girl. He went on to say that he would also like to have 11 sons.

I said I thought this was quite a lot, but he added that he wanted his own cricket team. Clearly, this would be a big ask of his other half. Out here, however, she would just be expected to get on with it. Refusing is not really an option. I believe that in an Afghan marriage, female consent is not a prerequisite for any baby-making activities. Pitying his poor wife, I asked if there were any options for spreading the load a bit. He responded that in his culture, he could have up to four wives provided he can support them all.

I asked him if he intended to have four wives. He said he was considering it. Blimey, I thought, some men are suckers for punishment.

19th October 2011: Finest Chefs in the World

Folks on the base, in order to break up the culinary tedium, will, when the opportunity arises, try and eat in an alternative cookhouse or, as the yanks call it, "DEFAC".

These "dining facilities" will be located at other posts, and because the incumbent contractor is likely to be different, the menus will reflect that. It is said that on a US Base, they pay more per head for their food than on a NATO base.

An obvious manifestation of this is Ben and Jerry's ice cream rather than the softly whipped pottage we get here. However, if it is an American base, you will tire of the offering quite promptly and yearn for good old British grub like curry. Without a doubt, the best scoff in the entire Theatre can be found in the British Army cookhouse at Camp Bastion.

The food is just like mother makes, albeit mum perhaps doesn't resemble a 40-year-old Indian gentleman with a nice line in pidgin English. Still, the folks who supervise the food preparation through monitoring the contract are the finest chefs in the world, namely British Army cooks. However, Camp Bastion is a long way away, so the best option for varying your gastronomic fare is to walk to another base nearby.

If I'm there working, I'll eat in its cookhouse, but unlike others, I'll not tab there just for the sake of a meal. The vast majority of folks on that base are Americans, and the base is named after one of their fallen soldiers. It's all paper plates and plastic cutlery. There is, however, one exception to this rule. As we queue at the hot plate, we all pass a private place setting for one.

This consists of a red tablecloth upon which sits a china plate, stainless steel cutlery and a wine glass. Accompanying this place setting is a vase with a single rose in it. There is no food or drink, and nobody sits there. It's been laid in honour of the lad who was killed, and after which the base is named.

20th October 2011: Exposed

In the British Army, we call it a "chuff chart". It's a mechanism for monitoring how many days you have served and, therefore, more importantly, how many days you have remaining.

For most folks, a simple calendar suffices, but others make up some kind of chart. I have never bothered. Firstly, doing so reminds me that I am, in fact, away, and secondly, you can never trust the Army. It would be soul-destroying just as you are crossing out the last few days only to be told to suck it up, cupcake you've got to stag on.

Some believe the days go quickly, whereas the weeks go slowly. Others say it's the reverse. All I know is that it feels as if I've been here for years, and every time I wake up I'm still here. That said, I've got it easy. I'm on a six-month tour that will, all being well, be finished after six and half months.

On the other hand, the US Army stags on for twelve months. They get a mid-tour break of two weeks. There is, however, some good news for the Americans in that for new arrivals, their tour length will be reduced to nine months. Indeed 12-month tours are not unique as full Colonels and above in the British Army also do them. This is one example

I can think of where rank having its privilege is turned on its head.

Returning to my theme of the "chuff chart" I have noticed that one officer has gone all high tech. One of the Dutchmen has an application on his computer, which calculates how much of a picture should be revealed each day, dependent on the duration of his tour.

When the picture is fully "exposed", he's out of here. Him being Dutch means I don't need to tell you what the picture is. But if you need a clue, it is not a pair of clogs, windmill or polder. The word "exposed" should also be a hint.

21st October 2011: Mr You Buy

He was about seven and sat with his mother on the side of the road. She was making her daily supplications towards Mecca, bowing backwards and forward; her prayer mat dusty from the street. The little lad was busying himself with a bowl of rice the trinkets displayed on a rug to his side.

He spotted me coming and stood up quickly, casting a cloth over his bowl to stop the flies from getting at it. His aim was slightly off, and there was a slender gap. He glanced back at the bowl as if to make a better job of it but hesitated as he could see I was moving at pace. He left his bowl, scooped up some bangles and ran after me.

"Mr, you buy."

"No thanks, son."

His eyes would have lit up a coal mine, and his smile could have driven away winter. If needed, my mother would have fostered him in a heartbeat; such was his charm. Despite the disappointment of not making a sale, his face was still full of joy.

"Here, have a sweet."

'Oh . . . thank you. What about my mother?"

"Here's one for her too."

"And my brother?"

I was figuring he was a sharp little mite, and another sweet was pressed into his palm.

"And my father?" He knew he was pushing his luck, but I admired him for his neck.

How many fathers do you have?" I asked him somewhat mischievously.

"Four," he responded and gave me a look as if to say he thought I might just buy it. I gave him one more sweet and then ushered him away from the traffic.

He walked back to his mum, satisfied with his raid on this particular soldier. She, however, continued in her dedications, oblivious to the encounter.

22nd October 2011: Three-Star General

If you like 4x4s, you'll love it here. It's the preferred mode of transport for those in this neck of the woods. They are, however, nothing like what you would see at home.

For a kick-off, they are American in their dimensions and secondly, they are so full of armour that it's more a case of gallons per mile than miles per gallon. Moreover, for some reason, which I have yet to fathom, they do not have number plates. They do, however, have cards, which indicate how important the passenger is. These cards sit where we would put our tax disc. As the windows are darkened, you cannot really see who is travelling inside. I think on one occasion, I was a Three-Star General because the driver had "inadvertently" left the card in place.

As a road safety precaution, when on base, every vehicle has to be led. This means that somebody has to walk in front to control the vehicle's speed and to warn pedestrians. Occasionally in order to speed things up, some vehicle guides have chosen to run instead.

This takes the vehicle that is following over the speed limit, which has attracted the ire of the Base Commander. Those guilty of such a measure have been threatened with all sorts. This approach of leading a vehicle is a sensible road safety policy, and it has reduced the odd bump. It is, however, strange to have a vehicle crawl up alongside you, nice and slow. I'm half expecting some geezer to lean out the window and ask me what I charge or make some other smart remark.

I've already tucked away some choice responses, but I will not share them with you, as I know my reader in the Green Man has a delicate disposition. One of them, however, does involve a reference to an assault rifle and a part of one's anatomy.

23rd October 2011: Daddy Will Be Coming Home for Christmas

The Deputy Commander of this gaggle of underachievers wanted a laydown of who was going on leave and when. He also wanted to know when we were being replaced. My team was up with the hunt, less our new Dutchman who had yet to identify his R&R.

"Sir, when can I take my leave?" he enquired.

"Take Christmas and the New Year off," I responded.

He looked at me with an expression of complete surprise, so I got in first.

"Look, I'm off in November, the laughing Dutchman is off now, and the Sergeant Major is going early next year. The best slot for you is the Christmas period, and besides, the work tempo should ease off a bit."

I could see he was troubled by the prospect of going home over Christmas while the rest of us remained here, so I had to expand on my justification.

"Moreover, this is not your first tour in Afghanistan, and besides, the boys would be happier in the knowledge that at least one of us will get home for Christmas."

Later I signed his leave pass, and as I did so, I looked at a picture of his wife and two young children. Your daddy will be coming home for Christmas, I thought, and that made me happy.

24th October 2011: Maritime Ensign

On deploying to Afghanistan, I made a point of not taking any personnel effects because my ruck and grip already weighed a ton. I did, however, make an exception for a photo album of my family and a harbour ensign.

The ensign used to fly on my ship and has been with me in the Balkans, Northern Ireland, Iraq and now Afghanistan. I am enormously attached to it and fully expect it to be placed in my coffin when I make my final voyage. I was subsequently deeply moved when a group of American soldiers took it with them back to their base and ran it up their flagpole.

In addition, they mustered as a body and had a photograph taken of themselves with the flag. I have copied the pictures to some of the lads I was at sea with, and I'm pleased to note that these photographs now sit on my Regiment's Facebook site. I think this is one of the rare occasions when a maritime ensign has flown in Afghanistan, which, as you know, is landlocked.

It was a lovely gesture by the Americans, and I am very grateful to them. It almost makes up for the chewing tobacco debacle. Well, perhaps not.

25th October 2011: Appropriate Attire

No good deed goes unnoticed. It seems that I'm not the only one who has the occasional banter with the children outside the camp gate. More nefarious groups of youths have taken note of this interaction and seen it as an opportunity to enrich themselves.

There have been reports of pickpockets and females being touched. One lass found herself sidled up to in the dusk and, as a consequence, felt it necessary to draw her pistol and threaten to shoot her groper. She was so upset by the incident that she handed her weapon and ammunition into the armoury on the grounds that she didn't want to kill anyone.

I can't quite understand how this could have occurred because she would not have been alone. That said, it appears to have happened. Being an American, the handing in of your personal weapon is not an option, so she was made to take it back. I know I am in dangerous territory here, but some young ladies working with civilian agencies do dress somewhat provocatively.

While this habit is confined to the base, we are nevertheless surrounded by young Afghan males for whom this must be rather overwhelming. While High Command does remind people as to what is appropriate attire, some quarters do appear to give it a stiff ignoring. I did hear a female officer complain about the standards of dress adopted by some of her gender.

With so many testosterone-fuelled young men being separated from their amours, she thought it was extremely inconsiderate to excite them so.

This would also explain the Padre's excellent but regular sermon on the sins of adultery. For the old fat knackers like me, such concerns are long past. A colleague did ask me somewhat tongue in cheek if I was worried about being groped when exiting the base on a Thursday. I replied that I had no such worries. After all, I'm that ugly my wife wouldn't even contemplate the idea.

26th October 2011: Aromatic Outrage

The offering looked decidedly tasty as we filed past the hot plate in an orderly fashion. In a failure of literary imagination, however, the chef had described it simply as "cabbage roll".

It deserved a better sobriquet but nevertheless flew off the hot plate. It consisted of what resembled a sausage meat core tightly enveloped in cabbage leaves and baked in the manner of a roast. It was, however, excellent and being the vegetarian choice, it was generally considered a healthy option. The after-effects, however, were less so.

The full realisation of this culinary offensive didn't become apparent until later. As the three of us slaved away in our container, which passes for an office, the General stepped in. Being disciplined troops, we stood to attention, which must have disturbed the natural disposition of the airflow within the room. The noxious onslaught was immediate. The General mumbled, stepped back and disappeared at pace.

The Deputy Commander, through barely suppressed giggles, demanded to know who had "gassed". The Sergeant Major flung open the window, and the Dutchman buried his head in his hands. Somebody blamed the dog. When it was realised we didn't have a dog, it was suggested that the cat was responsible. Even the mouse was lined up to take the rap.

Grabbing a can of air freshener, the Sergeant Major proceeded to hose down the room as the fan was put into overdrive. A call was terminated in the belief that we were being subjected to a biological attack. In an effort to restore order, I reminded my colleagues that this was hardly the battle of the Somme and that we should just calm down. The Dutchman, however, was not so sure. Eventually, the pandemonium subsided, and order was restored. The working environment then settled back down to a normal working routine.

The after-action report has recommended that we ban cabbage for lunch. As to who was responsible for this aromatic outrage, he is known only to God.

27th October 2011: Living the Dream

"Good morning Jim," I announced in a chirpy voice.

"It isn't that," he responded.

His depressing riposte may have been because it was 05:30 in the morning or because he'd only been here for a few days. The more usual reply is: "Living the dream".

I haven't quite worked out what that dream is yet. If it is what I think it is, then I'm not enjoying living it. This is now my fourth consecutive month without a day off, and I'm beginning to flag. Were I working for the Foreign and Commonwealth Office, I'd have had a month at home by now. Strangely enough, the advantageous conditions under which these civil servants work does not grate with me.

The thought of trooping off home every six weeks while the boys suffer at the forward operating bases doesn't somehow seem right.

All Vaccinations Are Voluntary

My general lethargy could, however, be due to my flu jab, which I had this morning. All vaccinations are voluntary, which I suspect is a consequence of the Human Rights Act.

However, not volunteering is deemed unprofessional. If a soldier goes down with an avoidable sickness, then he becomes an unnecessary burden on the medical chain and a liability to his mates who now have to cover for him. That said, when I saw this great huge bruiser of a Sergeant with his tattoo-enriched forearms, I was in the throes of changing my mind. However, he stepped aside to reveal a charming young Corporal who seemed to understand the inherent cowardice that lies within.

On receipt of said vaccination, I was told to remain in place for ten minutes and that I shouldn't take any exercise for at least 24-hours. I remarked that on previous occasions, I was told that I shouldn't drink either. The young lady said that she'd stopped saying that because the lads thought she was extracting the Michael.

I can understand why because, as I have already reported, there is not a drop to drink out here. Unless, of course, you are a civil servant working for the Foreign and Commonwealth office where I suspect you are allowed to sup in the privacy of your own room. As to supping, I can already taste the six pints of real ale waiting for me behind the bar of my favourite watering hole. My regular reader will know immediately that I am referring to the Green Man.

I'm also extremely grateful to the gentleman who has shown such generosity by paying for this ale. He being late RAF suggests it is indeed a kindness. That he has extended such largesse to this particular "Pongo" speaks well of his character. Pongo, for those who don't know, is military slang for a soldier. It is based on the observation that where the Army goes, the pong goes, and there are certainly a few pongs around here.

28th October 2011: Little Malingering

People drive themselves hard here. A while ago, our American General complained of a splitting headache, and although he tried to work through, it was obvious he was going down with something. Reluctantly he went to the quack and returned three days later clearly still unwell, but his pride had forced him back to the office.

Our new General also went belly up and was hospitalised for a number of days. Sadly, he has had to return once more to the infirmary. He'd obviously forced himself back to work before he had fully recovered.

I'd noticed the Sergeant Major was driving himself too hard also. He was trying to do all things for all men. The other morning, he looked quite pale and for someone whose dad is an African American. I figured he must be sick.

"Sergeant Major, go to bed and get some rest," I insisted.

Even he'd worked out that this was good advice, so off he trooped. The following morning, he shows up looking like death with a hangover.

"Sergeant Major, what are you doing here?" which frankly was a rhetorical question.

"Go back to bed," I added.

He wasn't for budging, so the General told him to go and rest.

Later I caught him going to bible class which, whilst not strictly working, was nevertheless not resting. So, we had more words.

I read recently that MoD civil servants take an average of eight days off sick a year. I'm sure it's a reflection of our times, but it is nevertheless quite a contrast to what I see out here. Having a General practically order a man to take to his bed suggests there is little malingering. Turning up for work when you feel like death warmed up shows dedication. The boss can always send you home if there is a risk of infection. This attitude is called "duty", and it is humbling to see it in action.

29th October 2011: I Pray That I Get Through

"Warning: You are making a non-secure call. Loose talk may put your comrades in danger. Welcome to paradigm services. Calls made using this device may be monitored for security. To use your account card, press one. If you are using a disposable card, press two."

Any welfare call back to the UK is always preceded by the above message. Not only may the Taliban be listening in but also our own security services. It puts a bit of a damper on any thoughts as to a romantic conversation.

When I call home, I'm half expecting the Taliban to butt in and ask after the chickens, and I'm sure the security services are fascinated by my exhortations to work hard at school.

Sadly, there is a need for them to eves drop.

When one of our soldiers is killed, the ability to make welfare calls is denied. The process for doing so is known as Op Minimise. This is done to prevent the family of the deceased being notified unofficially. If that were to happen, the military wouldn't have time to put in place all the necessary welfare support.

On one occasion, I couldn't get through because of Op Minimise. I felt frustrated and then had a word with myself for being so selfish. My being inconvenienced was nothing compared to the reason why. Now when I ring home, I pray that I get through. Not necessarily because of a desire to speak to loved ones but because it means we haven't lost another soldier.

30th October 2011: It Counted for Nothing

I'd gazed at the behemoth in awe as it crawled carefully through the base. This ironclad on wheels was a sight to behold. Named Rhino, its metal bulk gave it a size and sense entirely in keeping with its mammalian namesake.

It looked awesome, secure, reliable and safe. It counted for nothing as a Taliban car bomb ripped through it yesterday, killing some thirteen of those on board. I know a lot about the Rhino because I'd looked at using it to get to some place where I was needed, but I opted for another method.

There was a gathering of folk in church, and the memorial candle on the altar was lit. I didn't notice the Chaplain, but I imagine he had more pressing business. The other day he mentioned that nobody was offering him spiritual support and that he needed it. On Friday, he was at a camp for internally displaced refugees. The Sergeant Major had gone with him.

I think I know the Sergeant Major well enough to suggest he could take a life in a blink of an eye, and yet there he was explaining that he had tears in his eyes on seeing the distress of these people. Afghans with canes shepherded them forward to receive the largess of these western Christians. There were very young girls holding babies that were not their siblings.

This human destitution will have upset the Chaplain, and the loss of the Rhino bus will have added to his distress. It comes to something when you are praying for your priest to keep it together.

It was nice of the BBC to report the incident to the world before folks at home knew whether or not their loved ones were on board. I now understand the lyrics of that Jam hit "The public gets what the public wants". That said, in watching the BBC reporting, it occurred to me that I may have known somebody on board. I gave him a call.

The deep southern drawl told me he was alright. Well, sort of. Where he was operating, three Australians had been killed.

31st October 2011: Dear Holly's class

Thank you very much for all your lovely letters, which arrived yesterday. The drawings are wonderful. You have all gone to a lot of trouble, and I have thoroughly enjoyed reading them.

To Toby, I would like to say that the Afghan children do have some toys, and yes, they do speak to me. I do not, however, have a double-barrel shotgun.

To my niece, I would say that I have two guns, which I have to clean occasionally. I loved the picture of the tank.

Like you, Isaac, I, too, am a Saints fan. As you know, the Saints are the best rugby team in the country and say hello to your best friend Ewan for me. Your tank is also a nice picture, as is the Saints' rugby player.

Congratulations on your birthday in September, Felicity, your presents sound great. You, too, asked after the children, and while they are poor, they seem happy. Your trampoline sounds great but be careful with all your front flips. They sound a bit tricky.

I, too, like gobstoppers and say hello to your brother and sister. I'm glad you are learning about World War II,

Isabella, and your picture of a tank suggests you are learning fast. It is not nice fighting in Afghanistan, and yes, I have been bitten by a mosquito, but I take tablets to stop malaria. The picture of me shooting a Taliban while wearing my medals is very colourful. I am so happy that you didn't draw the Taliban shooting back.

Like you, Eleanor, I too hate the war in Afghanistan, but sometimes it is necessary when bad people have guns. It is unpleasant in the war and sometimes as you suggest it is a bit scary. I see plenty of children and give them sweets. This is naughty, I know, as you shouldn't accept sweets from strangers.

But when I do give them sweets, there is always a policeman watching. Some but not all go to school, and yes, some have school uniforms, which are blue. I enjoy talking to the children. I do miss my family and friends, and no, I haven't been injured but thank you for asking. I have several medals and am due to get a couple more. Your picture of one of my medals is very nice.

I am glad Emily that you are a friend of my niece and you must be very excited about getting a horse. They do have animals in Afghanistan, and yes, I see the children occasionally, some of whom are riding on carts being pulled by donkeys.

I am pleased, Ethan, that your house which you have made has not been bombed in your school project. Your picture of the tank is very colourful, as it is of the soldiers. I note that one is smoking a cigarette, which cannot be good for him, although the bullets might be a bigger problem.

I do have a hobby Maya, which is bell ringing, although I am not very good at it. It's nice that you should ask about my hobby and I hope you continue to enjoy your horse riding. Sadly, I do not know the children's names, but I shall ask. I like your picture of a Pop Party. The stars are very pretty. I'm not a big fan of chewing gum because it gets stuck in my teeth.

It is great that you like reading Isabella, and I have a daughter who is also a fan of Harry Potter. Your pets are very interesting, and I am sorry you do not like gas masks. They fit much better today, unlike during World War II. I see you have dressed up as an evacuee.

Thank you, Lauren, for saying my niece is really nice. I think so too. I think that learning is cool too. Not all of the children in Afghanistan are OK, but a lot of good people are trying to help them.

Yes, Jack from Deanshanger, the children do talk to me, and I liked making dens when I was your age too. I have four medals, but I have left them back in England. The weather was very, very hot in the summer but it is cooler now. I like the children in Afghanistan. Your self-portrait is very good, as is the picture of a tank.

Well, Ben, you having millions of questions would keep me a little busy, but I will answer the ones you have asked. The war in Afghanistan started when some bad people made their home here, and the people who lived here let them stay. I have seen lots of children, and yes, I have talked to them.

They speak some English but, in their country, they speak Dari. I'm glad you are excited about seeing if I reply, and I hope you like my answers. Your picture of a rug, volleyball and self-portrait all in green are splendid.

The picture of a house being bombed that was drawn by William shows all the bricks and the roof going skyward. I, too, am really interested in war but now think I need to specialise in avoiding them. I like history too, William, and I think I have some of the horrible history books at home.

I'm not sure Bessy what it is like to be nearly in charge of everyone. I am in charge of some people but not that many. Do have a lovely time in Hamburg watching football with your dad. The food is OK, but I wouldn't say it was nice. I'm glad, Bessy, that you asked me to please turn over, as all the pictures are terrific. Do be careful doing handstands, and yes, I do have some pets, which are chickens.

I love rugby too, Miles, but I'm not very good at football. As for how I feel, thank you for asking. I feel much better for having received all these kind letters.

Great picture of a medal and an aeroplane.

Daniel, you are right, books are brilliant, and as for your picture of the Army coming home, that is just fantastic. You show them coming home by sea and air. Your tank has lots of wheels, which must have taken an age to draw; well done.

I have not seen the TV programme Bears' Behaving Badly, Samantha, but I'm sure it is great. You hate the war in Afghanistan, too, and ask what it is like fighting. At my age, I tend not to do the fighting, but I meet lots of people who do. It is not very nice. I love the union flag and the medal picture Samantha.

Thank you for writing, Ewan, and yes, I do have two children. Thank you for asking. East Claydon is a lovely village, and you must enjoy living there. Football is a great game, but I was never really very good at it. Your picture of you in a football strip is superb.

It is kind of you, Jake, to thank me for defending us English. It is really appreciated. Playing pretend armies must be good fun, especially as you live in a rural area. When you grow up, you can join the real Army, but hopefully, by then, wars will be over, and you will not need to.

Can I finish by saying to you all how much I loved your letters? And to my niece Holly what I would add is that you have a lovely group of class friends. Do enjoy the street parties and the dressing up as evacuees that so many of you wrote about. Finally, I would like to finish by saying a big thank you to your teacher who must have been very busy with all your fantastic letters.

Love from Holly's uncle

November 2011: Our Jack And Me (Part 1)

There was a whoosh, a roar and a shout,
My mate Jack sends: "Contact Wait Out".
And Troopee's lost in a cloud of dust,
As the Taliban have our position sussed.

My mate Jack was on the radio,
Talking to some jet jockey called "Foxtrot Joe".
That's all I remember as I hit the dirt,
That and the stain growing on my shirt.

Will people pray for us on Remembrance Day,
Back at home in celebrity obsessed UK?
Or will they simply flick to Sky TV,
And give no thought to Jack and me.

Or will they part with the price of a beer,
And the chink of coins for a poppy seller's ear?
Now my widow's tears will not stop for this kind care,
But it will help Jack's mum buy him a wheelchair.

One dead soldier and one amputee,
The price paid by us for Afghan liberty.
One dead soldier and one amputee,
Were the chink of coins from our Jack and me.

Our Jack And Me (Part 2)

On Remembrance Day,
For whom did you pray?
Was it for me, or was it for Jack,
Or was it to have David Beckham back?

1st November 2011: Considered Reckless

"You all right cock?" I enquired of a naval Commander who seemed to be somewhat at a loss. It appeared he'd been locked out of his cell.

Being a sailor, he had a regular routine that involved starting promptly in the gym at 05:30. He'd done this for weeks now and had become accustomed to his RAF cellmate continuing with his unencumbered slumbers. That being so, our intrepid mariner stopped taking his room key with him to the gym.

There was no need to because on returning to his cell, he'd then wake the still sleeping crab. Crab is military slang for a person of RAF vintage. On this occasion, however, for reasons unknown, his RAF colleague decided that an early rise was in order and promptly locked the door as he'd left. Our commander couldn't locate him, which was a bit of a pain as he was to soon meet a commodore.

Rocking up in sweaty gym kit having been locked out of his cell wouldn't enhance his professional allure. Still, we managed to get things sorted, and events panned out okay. To my embarrassment, I had managed this feat of incompetence twice and subsequently had to locate my cellmate in order to use his key.

It does beggar belief, though. We can be trusted to look after our weapons and ammunition and to make decisions as to whether somebody needs to be shot or not, but to issue us with a spare key is clearly considered reckless.

2nd November 2011: The French Didn't Think So

We wear lots of badges on our uniform. Formation badges, skill at arms badges, rank slides, national flags, tactical recognition flashes ... the list goes on.

The base tailor must be making a fortune stitching them onto our battle dress. In the British Army, at least, all badges have to be endorsed by the relevant Regimental dress committees. These important bodies will also decide where the badges will be sited. After all, you cannot just stitch them on anywhere you like. That would be very unmilitary. However, new combat attire is being issued at such a pace I don't think the dress committees are keeping up.

This is especially so with the introduction of Velcro, which means badges can migrate about the uniform with ease. This is noticeably so regarding the "underbody armour shirts". Nevertheless, we Brits do keep a sense of proportion in these matters, and we do not kick the backside out of it.

Was this only true of our Kiwi brethren? They have knocked up a new badge, which they now wear on their shirtsleeves. It consists of a silhouette of the Webb Ellis Cup with two dates embroidered underneath. These dates are "1987" and "2011". I am pretty sure that this is entirely unofficial. However, as most of the Kiwis are Special Forces, I, for one, am keeping well and truly stum.

Especially as they resemble the All Blacks in both stature and hairstyle, I did cough the remark that the badges looked very stylish only to be told that the French didn't think so. To an Englishman, that is a nice touch, and I know of at least one Kiwi patron of the Green Man who will want me to source said emblem. I'm doing my best, but they are awesome lads. I can assure you mugging one of them for the badge is not an option.

3rd November 2011: Chairman Cloggie

There has been an improvement in the morale of this particular gathering of the daft and desperate who thought a career in the Armed Forces was a sensible course of action. The laughing Dutchman has returned to duty and already regaled us with stories of his less than incident-free return.

Over a coffee, at the airhead, while waiting for their transport, he had an immediate sinking feeling when his travelling companion remarked that he needed to go back to the arrivals to collect his bag. When they showed up, there were a number of burly troops manning a cordon.

"I think I may be the cause of the problem," explained his now worried mate. The US soldier was focused on ensuring people did not come any closer and wasn't overly interested in the thoughts of Chairman Cloggie. Sometime later, via the Military Police, events came to a conclusion.

The lost bag had been destroyed in situ by a small explosive charge rendering the contents kaput. It seems that a combination of a pillow, mobile phone, assorted garments and a laptop charger, blended in with a packet of Belgian waffles, made for an interesting outcome. The EOD boys like blowing things up, so I'm not sure they were that bothered. High Command, however, and a lot of inconvenienced soldiers, will, of course, have a different view. Were there a bar here, he would now be bankrupt for having to make amends through the purchase of beer.

4th November 2011: Bothered the Sergeant Major

I do not have enough fingers and toes to count our recent dead. Our base is now in lockdown, with those going out on the ground needing a pass signed by their General.

I have decided not to bother mine partly because he is in hospital having medical treatment and partly because I'm distinctly off the idea of going clubbing downtown. This, however, does mean our C of E Padre will not be visiting in order to take the morning service.

Our on-base Pentecostal Chaplain has kindly agreed to step in. He has done this before, and I know he finds our more formal approach somewhat constraining. Whether or not it's because he is a Latino, I have no idea, but he is far more demonstrative than the elders of St Mary's would be accustomed to. With our young lads going out on patrol in the more dangerous parts of Helmand, you could argue that our Chaplain should just ignore the risks and come on over.

I was minded to think that until I realised that it would be those same lads who would be bringing him. The gutsy little blighters wouldn't hesitate, so I am happy for a little more funk than usual in my worship. I use the words 'lads' in an inclusive sense. The doctor who was reported to have

302

been killed in the Rhino bus bombing, being a Lieutenant Colonel, was hardly a lad, nor was the 19-year-old girl blown up in another IED attack.

I know the latter death bothered the Sergeant Major because he mentioned it. In his eyes, she was still a child and being a reservist on active duty was perhaps still adapting to the enormity of what she faced. It must be my age, but whilst I am humbled by these girls and hold my manhood cheap in their presence, the thought of sending teenage girls to war somehow doesn't sit well with me.

Plus Ca Change

I mentioned to a colleague that I hadn't seen his "oppo" in a while. I was told he was constantly working and barely out of the office. As a bomb doctor, he is trying to counter these improvised explosive devices and therefore save the lives of our soldiers.

Every death will drive him on. His measures of performance are too stark for words. No wonder he is unable to rest. His great uncle would have been proud of him but no doubt disappointed that despite his efforts, a descendent would once more be in Afghanistan. Plus ca change, as the French would say, albeit with a better accent.

303

5th November 2011: Still a National Event

Our National Support Element is now selling poppies, which are starting to appear on our uniforms. The Canadians are doing likewise. Their poppies, however, are slightly different but have the same meaning.

Details of our remembrance services have been promulgated, and we have been told to ensure we have a poppy on the day. Many of the lads wear their "Help for Heroes" wristbands throughout the year, and the poppy is a colourful addition. The Americans wear a similar wristband, although theirs reads "Wounded Warrior".

The principle is the same, which is to raise funds for wounded soldiers. I have seen some Brits wearing an American wristband along with our own and seen Americans doing likewise. It's a nice touch and much appreciated. Indeed, the all American Sergeant Major is very proud of having done a charity run for "Help for Heroes".

It doesn't bother me not seeing folks wearing a poppy when I'm at home. Thanks to our soldiers, we live in a free country, and when people choose not to wear a poppy, it is a reminder that they have a choice. A choice provided ironically by the very soldiers who they choose not to recognise. I'm also aware that sometimes one is bereft of a poppy because it gets left on another garment, and it can be a fiddly accoutrement.

Poppy wearing belongs to no particular class, faith or culture. I recollect seeing a Goth dressed in statutory black with face piercings and spiky hair proudly sporting her poppy. I do, however, get slightly irritated at Jon Snow's annual refusal to wear a poppy while presenting Channel 4 news. He certainly has a choice, but as Channel 4 is, I believe, subsidised by the taxpayer, he should perhaps recognise what is still a national event.

More a Thinker

Towing the party line, as it were, has relevance today with the announcement in the world media that one of our American Generals has been sacked. I knew him reasonably well and had the honour of spending ten minutes with him in a one on one conversation whilst waiting for transport.

He was a huge man yet quietly spoken. He was not the Rambo type; more a thinker. He had my respect, and nothing in his going has changed that; quite the contrary, in fact. My

Mum had never told me that speaking candidly could get you sacked but it clearly can out here.

6th November 2011: Pending Your Questions Sir, that Concludes My Brief

I sent the following to the Deputy Commander of my branch as a proposal for when I'm next required to brief at the stand up:

Good morning Sir,

My name is Lieutenant Colonel Overworked, and in the next few minutes, I'm going to brief you about an issue facing the command.

NEXT SLIDE, PLEASE.

This slide, while resembling a Chinese guard report, is designed to outline the problem. It is full of bright colours and peppered with numbers, which makes the whole thing unintelligible. It does, however, allow me to prove to you my credentials as a PowerPoint ranger.

NEXT SLIDE, PLEASE.

This slide is equally confusing, but you will note how clever I am in having pop-ups and words pinging in from the side. You must now be overwhelmed by the luminosity of my creativity. I am sure you can deduce that what this slide depicts is the background to the issue. This, however, is a supplementary concern as my primary purpose is to impress you with my command of PowerPoint.

NEXT SLIDE, PLEASE

My final slide is designed to confirm in your mind that I am a first-class PowerPoint guru. Note the clever use of shading and tiny photographs that I have skillfully incorporated into this cacophony of colour. You must agree that overall, this entire slide is a work of artistic brilliance. I wouldn't be too bothered at not quite understanding what my proposed solution is, but you have got to admit it's a belter of a slide.

NEXT SLIDE, PLEASE

Pending your questions, sir, that concludes my brief. I trust you are suitably impressed.

The above draft has been circulated to some within the headquarters for their amusement. I hope I don't get into trouble. I'll find out soon enough when I return from R&R in late November.

Crab Air

To my reader in the Green Man who has kept up with my jottings, I would just say that my next missive will be on or about 26th November. It will be on or about because I'll be flying home in the care of the RAF.

For those of you who haven't flown Crab Air, it resembles a no thrills airline during an Air Traffic Controllers dispute underpinned by an Icelandic eruption. That said, they are efficient. On the last occasion, I was ordered to open my bag as the inspecting NCO thought I was smuggling a bottle of port. He was a polite chap only doing his duty. He didn't, however, fancy a swig ... it was a bottle of TCP.

8th November 2011: It will be Their Last Meal

Having announced that my next missive would be on or about 26th November, I find myself at a loose end stuck in a main operating base waiting to get on a flight home.

I left in good order yesterday evening all dressed up in my Robocop kit and was moved in a vehicle packet to another location near to the airhead. My travelling companion was an RAF Squadron Leader who advised me not to overnight there but to press on that evening.

This sounded a favourable option, so I stopped long enough just to get a meal. This was at a British base with a British run cookhouse. The RAF lad had said that the food was outstanding, and for an RAF officer to say that, then you know it must be good. After all, they considered lobster a food for the masses. The only downer he said was that there was no crockery, and it was all paper plates and plastic cutlery.

Frankly, I was blown away by the quality of the food. We Brits do feed our soldiers extremely well, and my plastic cutlery had no trouble dealing with the steak I'd had cooked to order. After scoff (food), we again formed up for the onward move. This vehicle packet consisted of a different vehicle type, which had a television in the back.

As I settled down to watch BBC News, I was, of course, disappointed. The six channels were infrared views from various aspects of the vehicle.

The dog was the most interesting amusement other than that the in-house entertainment needed working on. It was late when we arrived, and funny old thing, there were plenty of seats available on the aircraft. This may be due to the fact that midnight beckoned.

I say seats, they were, in fact, canvas benches, and we were once more all togged up in our battle rattle. It seemed unusual nestling amongst your fellow air travellers to find they were armed to the teeth with a plethora of assault weapons. My ear defenders kept most of the noise out as we trundled over Afghanistan. I use the word "trundle" as there was a bit of turbulence.

When we arrived at the main operating base, I tried my luck on a connecting aircraft to the UK. No such luck, so we were bussed to what I would describe as tented accommodation but is more formally known as temporary deployed accommodation. The base was busy, and it was something like a James Bond film without the love interest. The ground was like cement powder rather than sand, and there was fine dust everywhere.

The Corporal assigned us to our accommodation, so off we plodded. Having rolled our sleeping bags out, we were soon in a deep sleep until a crowd of soldiers arrived suitably knackered. I did ask if they were bringing a cup of tea. As this is a family read, I cannot print the response. Later on, I shall make another attempt at flying home early.

Again, I am at a British run facility, and the food is excellent. I recollect asking a British Army cook why the food was so good. She told me it's because, for some of the lads, it will be their last meal.

9th November 2011: The RAF were Superb

My attempt at getting an earlier flight home proved successful. We were told to report to the airhead and wait for the flight manifest to be processed, after which if there were any spare seats, we would be called forward. There was a young NCO who was also hoping to catch an earlier flight.

He was, I think, disappointed at seeing me. I suspect he feared that if there was only one spare seat, I'd be allocated it due to rank. Well, rank has its responsibilities, so I told him if that was the case, he'd be on it, and I'd wait for the next flight. As it happens, there were several spare seats, so we both dipped in. Whilst I would not want this to be public knowledge because it would compromise the reputation that the Army has for the RAF, I have to confess that much as it grates me to say it, the RAF was superb.

That said, they still have the return flight to revert to type. The Tri-Star took off at dark o'clock. I was surrounded by infantry who were only too keen to get home after a six-month tour. There was also a soldier who was flying home on compassionate grounds, and for whom the trip could not pass quickly enough. He'd been assigned a young officer to accompany him on the flight. She was only a slip of a girl who coincidentally had been brought up in the same village as me. She was that small I could carry her under one arm, but I would have needed a fleet of trucks to carry her courage.

She was returning to the UK on R& R and, in turn, would do the high threat explosive ordinance disposal officers' course, after which she would be back in Afghanistan taking on the Taliban bomb makers. There was a little bit of work on the prayer front needed there, I thought.

In that business, you only lose once, and when you do, the bomb maker has got it right. You don't get a second chance to get it wrong. For the bomb maker, failure is a lesson learned, so he simply improves on the design.

Where BA Puts Its Wealthy, the Military Puts Its Injured

As we boarded the plane, I noticed that in the front of the aircraft, there were high care beds instead of first and club class seats.

Where BA puts its wealthy, the military puts it injured. I'm sure there is something profound in that observation, but I cannot quite figure it out. If ever I am lucky enough to fly club class, this observation will considerably undermine the experience. Fortunately, on this occasion, all the beds were empty.

During the flight, I would watch the nurses meticulously checking their equipment. I found their attention to detail fascinating. This may have been because their conversations and sudden outbursts of laughter would wake me from my dozing. I didn't mind being disturbed.

There is something uplifting about young people laughing in each other's company. I should enjoy it. There will be no laughing when those beds are occupied.

(Home leave for two weeks)

27th November 2011: I Wish Colin Montgomerie Every Success

After being tipped into the care of the RAF at Brize Norton, I reported to the check-in as instructed. A very kind young airman told me I was too early and issued me with a chit, which entitled me to an overnight stay in the RAF's Gateway Hotel.

Despite the pretentious name, it was, in fact, transit accommodation with carpets. The luxury aspect was that I got my own room which I have to report had all the charm of a dislodged toilet seat. I pondered what a hotel inspector would make of it all and concluded that despite the excellent staff, the star criteria would not apply, but four exclamation marks just might.

The room was equipped with two single beds and a baby's cot, all fitted with plastic sheets, which says a lot for the modern soldier. Over the basin was a notice, which advised caution. This advice required personnel to run the taps for three minutes before use. Moreover, during this procedure, they were to avoid breathing in the aerosol spray.

I'm sure my medically trained fellow patron in the Green Man would understand why but I was at a loss. That said, I clearly failed to follow this most basic instruction as on filling the basin, I was faced with what resembled a bowl of diluted mulligatawny soup.

An earlier experience in the Army of sleeping in a horsebox during an escape and evasion exercise proved excellent preparation for the mattress. It wasn't long, however, before I fell into a deep sleep (aided by a pint of Guinness) only to be woken with a start by an Orwellian discourse emanating from a tannoy situated on the wall.

"We are waking you at 02:30 and not the planned 03:10 as the computer is down, requiring a manual check-in process. Please acknowledge by pressing the orange button."

Due to my comatose condition, I'm not sure I got this right and may have mumbled something into the light switch.

Breakfast was somewhat rushed, so I carried my coffee to the bus that was idling outside. The driver was having none of it, so my caffeine injection went for a burton. The lady at reception must have thought me kind for bringing her a coffee. The haste of my boarding necessitated me leaving it on her counter.

We checked in at a time that would see a milkman still abed and then waited to board the aircraft. Boarding, however, was delayed due to a technical failure which one wag remarked involved a pilot and his alarm clock. This was an erroneous assumption as when we embarked and then disembarked thirty minutes later, there were engineers all over the place.

The crew were apologetic, and several of us were sympathetic. After all, the aircraft was a lot older than most of its passengers. When the plane first soared under a starlit panoply, they too were but twinkles.

Finally, seven hours after being woken abruptly, we took off in the aeronautical equivalent of an Arthur Daley motor. Had I paid for my ticket, I would have declined the invitation to fly and asked for my money back. Not just because of the obvious unreliability issues but also alas the destination. Despite the departure board making it very clear where we were going, this appeared to be no more than a suggestion. No sooner had I eventually dozed off were we kicked off the aircraft in Cyprus. After the crew was changed, we were off again to a new and exciting destination, which was nowhere near where I wanted to be.

When we landed there, our onward flight amounted to nothing, and after spending a number of hours in an arrival lounge, we were bussed to some transit accommodation for an overnight kip, which amounted to no more than two hours and 30 minutes.

Some suggested we should simply remain in the arrival lounge, and frankly, this proposal was not without its merits. I would rate the transit accommodation as worse (five exclamation marks), and that is saying something. After all, the arrival lounge was not always used for such a purpose and is famous for being the last refuge of the Taliban before they were driven from the area.

I needed no leap of the imagination to believe that. Our subsequent connection took me to where I thought I was going on leaving RAF Brize Norton. As we boarded the Hercules, I was intrigued by the requirement to carry no sharp blades on the person, but guns with attendant charged magazines were permissible. I'm sure this is designed to inject humour into what would otherwise be a thoroughly miserable process.

After landing, I remained on the aircraft as we embarked further passengers for our final destination. I had an opportunity to engage one of them in conversation. I thanked him for his kindness in "swinging by" to boost the morale of our soldiers. I wanted to add that he probably felt quite at home, what with all the bunkers he'd seen. However, I thought that was perhaps a pun too far. He'd quickly cottoned on to my "swinging by" remark.

He had brought with him the Ryder Cup to show the boys. It was a splendid looking trophy guarded by a heavily built member of the RAF Regiment. I wish Colin Montgomerie every success in his future undertakings.

28th November 2011: Planning Another Invasion, Are We?

I arrived back at my place of work thoroughly knackered. I have concluded that the reason why flights into Theatre are so awful is to encourage military aggression because on arrival, I was ready to fight someone.

The first person I should bump into, however, was my General, who told me not to come into the office until the following morning. The sickner was I'd arrived back a day earlier than expected.

I promptly showed up in good order and was reassured by the efficiency of my khaki desperados. They had prepared a back to work brief, which they were keen to present. I was seriously impressed. Not only had they covered the key issues, but they had also anticipated my questions. Very slick and very professional. I was beginning to suspect they didn't need me until the deputy poked his head around the corner.

"Have you told him he is to brief the General at 16:30 today?"

I thought this was rather important and wondered why it had not been covered, and to my relief, this brief was presented to me with a flourish. When I glanced at Page 1, all was in order, but Page 2 was frankly a dog's breakfast, and it didn't improve with further reading.

"I can't brief this, it's SH one T," I exclaimed, with a degree of outrage.

I was then given the alternative version. They were having a laugh ... the little tinkers. As it happens, the brief went well.

Having now been made situationally aware, I hurried into the morning's briefing during which the Dutch General asked the German paratrooper what he thought was the smallest book in the world. The German told the General that he had no idea, to which the General responded that it was the German book of humour.

Our German paratrooper friend replied instantly that he had thought it was the Dutch Book of Military Victories. The meeting fell silent except for me, who burst out laughing as indeed did the Dutch General himself. Later on, I encountered the very same German paratrooper looking at a map of Norway.

"Planning another invasion, are we?"

If you are reading this posting, then I lived to tell the tale.

29th November 2011: Mo Sistas

The one thing that has struck me since I returned from R&R is that in my absence, several of my colleagues have started resembling the cast of the Village People pop group.

Not in dress, mind you, but in sporting a moustache. It seems that they have responded to the Movember campaign, which is being widely publicised by posters about the base. I know my Green Man reader will now be struggling to follow but put simply, a group of Aussies in Melbourne started a campaign to encourage clean-shaven men to grow moustaches in the month of November. This is being done in order to promote public awareness of prostate cancer and raise money accordingly.

A "Mos" is by all accounts Australian slang for a moustache and it being November gave rise to Movember. Anybody who takes on this challenge is referred to as a Mo Bro. They even have Mo Sistas (sic), who are girls that encourage men to be Mo Bros. I have to confess I thought initially that they too were in the tash growing business, but I'm saying nothing.

It's just as well that Royal Navy regulations forbid the growing of moustaches, as it could get quite tricky on man love Thursday. Especially considering the dress code of at least one member of the said pop group. The United States Navy, however, allows moustaches, so make of that what you will.

30th November 2011: The Lotus Position

I was told that I was looking stressed and needed to unwind a little. My Dutch colleagues insisted, therefore, that I joined them at their yoga class. I needed quite some persuading, I can tell you. Why on earth they'd taken up yoga during my absence on leave was a complete mystery to me until I saw the French instructor.

I had never done a yoga class before in my life and performed so badly I reckon I still haven't. The class was made up of Dutch, Americans, French, a Croat, an Italian, a Belgian, a bloke from Singapore and me. Mostly males, funny old thing. I managed the lotus position, after which things went from bad to worse. It would have been useful to have been a contortionist; such were the various postures asked of us by the instructor. The candles, I thought, were a bit of a fire hazard. The metallic bowl, which was struck before and after a period of meditation, made me think I was a Buddhist monk.

This may have been useful as I am convinced that there is no place for middle-aged Anglo-Saxon males in a yoga class. I did, however, manage a handstand with assistance. A Dutch colleague managed it solo, and I still haven't got over the sight of his hairy beer gut as the bottom of his T-shirt dropped down over his face.

Funny thing, though, I did feel a lot better for the yoga experience. To my reader in the Green Man who may be thinking of taking up yoga, I can highly recommend it. I certainly have a newfound respect for its practitioners.

December 2011: Santa's Sack

What is in Santa's sack,
Toys for kids and this and that?

What is in the Afghan sack,
Misery for soldiers and this and that?

So at the end of Christmas day,
When you put the toys away,
Give yourself a chance to pray,
For all our soldiers in harm's way.

1st December 2011: Intrusive Leadership

We have been advised that depression and suicide attempts are more prevalent during the winter holiday period. This guidance also included what signs we should be looking for.

It being dry out here, increased alcohol consumption was not one of them. Moreover, the missive counselled how we should address the subject when an individual showed those signs. Finally, we were asked to exercise "intrusive leadership".

I have always been a fan of this approach because unless you know personal details about people, how can you best support them? I am aware, however, that this would be considered a wildly inappropriate approach in civilian life.

Suicide is taken very seriously in the military, and sadly I have known one soldier took his own life. I found it painful when I learned of the incident. Still do. He had been one of my crew, and I was very fond of him as I was of all of them.

Suicide is an unwelcome relative of post-traumatic stress disorder (PTSD). Our training in this matter included the analogy that resistance to PTSD is like having a bank account. Some of us have a large resistance and, therefore, a healthy bank balance. Others have a lesser resistance and therefore, a smaller bank balance.

The key, though, is the rate of withdrawal. A strong balance will soon go into the red if there are several heavy withdrawals. By contrast, a lesser balance will be okay if the withdrawals are managed. The point being that PTSD can strike anyone, and it is not a sign of weakness. A colleague opened up to me that whilst in an area known as IED circle, a panic attack came on, and the individual wanted to rush from the vehicle. Being cocooned in an armoured car encased in body armour and helmet can be very claustrophobic, and it was this sensation that brought on the fear.

The emotion was compounded by the fact that the door could not be opened due to the stationary traffic. I inquired as to the cause of this vulnerability; Iraq by all accounts. It seems being subjected to six months of indirect fire and a 105mm artillery round partially detonating within 20 metres can be a little off-putting. Help though was being offered. The illness had been recognised.

The Deputy Commander of our staff branch, being mindful of the advice given regarding depression and suicide, did talk the policy through with me. I made the point that he needn't worry on my account. I would never give our Tory-led Coalition Government the satisfaction of saving on my redundancy package.

2nd December 2011: Your Hair will be the Correct Length for Cutting Next Thursday

I may have mentioned it before, but out here, we are entitled to one free haircut a month. To avail oneself of this service, one has to go to the National Support Element and see the Chief Clerk. This I did.

"Chief, may I have a chit for a hair cut please?"

"No, sir."

"Why on earth not?"

"Well, sir, according to the calendar, you are not due a haircut."

"But a haircut is dependent on the length of your hair, not the date."

"In that case, sir, your hair will be the correct length for cutting next Thursday. Come back then sir."

It's not as if a haircut, in my case, is particularly challenging. I threatened to grow a ponytail and promptly left. However, mention of my flight date home had me scurrying back in. This, too, was calendar-based. Were it to depend on mission success then; I may have problems.

332

3rd December 2011: The Red Book Variety

Diligent readers of my many lamentations will be pleased to know that nobody out here participated in the public sector day of action. Had any of us done so, a Court Martial would have beckoned.

The Armed Forces do not have the right to withdraw their labour. The event did, however, generate some heated comments in the cookhouse. Those officers, who supported the action, metaphorically speaking, were described as being of the red book variety and those who didn't the blue book. My political neutrality prevents me from hinting which tome I favoured. That well-known licence fee millionaire Jeremy Clarkson, entering the national debate, certainly added some spice.

The general view is that he was only joking, but, on some occasions, silence is good counsel. Of course, if he wishes to discuss the worth of public servants, I'm sure some of the boys who are about to go on a fighting patrol would be only too delighted to take him along. They can discuss the subject while tiptoeing through an alleyway laced with Improvised Explosive Devices (IEDs).

That said, we do know that Jeremy is a supporter of the Armed Forces who are, like teachers and nurses, public servants.

What has a British soldier and an Afghan got in common? They've both been shafted by their government ... well, it made me laugh.

4th December 2011: Considering their Rank, I Lost My Nerve

There were three Generals sitting in an office; a German General, a Polish General and a Dutch General. The joke was, I had to brief them on what my team does out here for a living.

The briefing went well, too well, in fact. The Command is looking to reduce numbers, and I doubt my successors will thank me for keeping them in a job. Perhaps I should have done them a favour and given the impression that my team wasn't needed. Had I done so, there was a chance they wouldn't have to come here. Let's hope nobody tells them.

Of course, the make-up of my audience had enormous scope for humour but considering their rank, I lost my nerve. I did, however, squeeze in the odd witty aside.

Strangely enough, the German was occupying the Pole's office having taken over from him. It's funny how history repeats itself. There is a certain irony about a German takeover of Polish property, but I wasn't bold enough to point that out.

5th December 2011: Aquatic Extravagance

I know that showers have now supplanted the bath in the public's affections for washing oneself down. That said, there is always a place for the good old soak, especially after a game of rugby. Sadly, there is no place out here for such a watery indulgence.

Well, at least I thought so until visiting a British Army base where I noticed a poster advertising the use of a bath in the medical centre. I have no idea why the sickbay should have a bath, but clearly, there is a therapeutic reason necessitating such an expense.

As I read this offer with increased enthusiasm, my anticipation was somewhat deflated by the realisation that this aquatic extravagance came with a price tag; five dollars, to be precise. Before my reader in the Green Man suspects war profiteering, I should add that any money raised would be going to charity. The poster also made it very clear that the nurses would not be offering any "additional services". I naturally assumed this to mean that one would have to provide one's own rubber duck.

6th December 2011: Breach of Food Labelling Regulations

He was happily chomping away through his curry while enjoying the convivial company of his colleagues. He was, however, not so engrossed in conversation as to miss the cockroach in his food.

He fished it out and then placed it on the side of his plate. That done, he continued with his meal, having not been bothered in the slightest. Well, he was a Marine. Having then finished his meal, he was minded to complain. Not because of the cockroach necessarily, but because it was a vegetarian curry that was obviously not. The debate then ensued that one cockroach hardly constituted a breach of food labelling regulations.

However, who is to say there wasn't more than one cockroach. Only finding one doesn't necessarily mean that there was only one. This then begs the question that if there were more, what happened to them? I think we all know the answer to that. Bon appétit.

7th December 2011: I Have a Sense of Kinship

It's not been a good couple of weeks. My reader in the Green Man will no doubt be following the recent incident involving Pakistan, which caused the death of so many of their soldiers.

As it happens, I occasionally take dinner with the Pakistan liaison officers, and we chat about all sorts of things. I suppose coming from Aylesbury, I have a sense of kinship. They speak of having had soldiers killed fighting the Taliban, and they talk with great compassion about their men.

Their being well informed, it is interesting to hear the Pakistani perspective on world affairs. One took a holiday recently in London and said he felt very welcome. This came as no surprise to me as I told him he'd find it like a home from home. Before he went, I reviewed his itinerary and, on his return, he thanked me for the trouble I'd gone to. I can understand why their Army is so dominant in Pakistani culture. Somebody, I suppose, has to have the wherewithal to step in when it all goes wrong.

These officers were heartbroken at the death of their countrymen and at a loss as to how it could have happened, and yet they were not angry, in the sense of wanting retribution, just disconsolate. As an aside, one did say it was nice to see a white face sitting chatting amongst them. He joins a long list of those who remarked when I was on leave that I'd not managed a tan.

Today, of course, another huge suicide bomb in Kabul. I was at a loss as to why I hadn't heard it. After all, I was only some 1200 metres away. But then I was in the cookhouse at the time, which is an extraordinarily noisy place to be.

8th December 2011: Going Price for a House

As we piled on through the streets, my attention was drawn by the range of houses we drove by. I asked the interpreter what the going price was for a house in Kabul.

He told me prices ranged from $40,000 to $400,000, which I thought was well within budget for England's second homeowners. These prices, mind, were for what we would recognise as houses. Stand fast the quality, but they would have piped water, albeit not necessarily taps, electricity and other amenities. The interpreter told me he lived in one valued at about $40,000 and could access freshwater from his home.

While house prices are out of reach in the UK for first-time buyers in their twenties, they are out of sight here. Indeed, that applies to most of the population. Those who could not afford houses would live in what the interpreter accepted were hovels. Most homes, however, would have electricity. That said, I can just imagine what Jet Set would make of the wiring. Still, it keeps the fire brigade in work.

The toilets would be improvised and emptied elsewhere, and the water sourced from a stand pump in the street, which would feed off a well; driven down into the aquifer. Many of these bothies were shacks on the mountainsides where land was available and fit for little else. The Afghans do have building regulations, but it seems they are not a priority, and over-enthusiastic inspectors can be bribed or threatened. By comparison, there is no housing shortage in the UK. I did not tell the interpreter that thousands of Englishmen have a second home for fear of upsetting him.

9th December 2011: Something Heart Warming

Words fail me. I'm speechless with delight. My faith in those who govern us has been given a major boost. I find myself proud of the behaviour of some of our politicians and now feel a little sheepish for my having held forth on so many occasions.

An oppo of mine has just returned, and the first question anybody ever asks is how the flights were. I was no different, and having asked the question, I then bathed in the responses with sympathetic gestures and words of solidarity. Like me, he too had been put through the wringer, but he had a wonderful tale to tell.

On leaving Theatre courtesy of the RAF, they fetched up in an airhead somewhere in the Middle East where the connecting flight home consisted of a chartered aircraft. Being chartered, it had two classes—business class to the front and cattle class to the rear.

Also travelling with Britain's finest were a large party of MPs who were returning from a fact-finding mission. They were from across the political spectrum, and their group included some peers. Whilst checking in, one of their numbers stepped forward and gave the instruction that the troops were to fly club class and the MPs would go cattle. Following their lead, the senior military officer announced that the soldiers would travel club class and the officers would fall in with the MPs. As it happens, the officers ended up with their men. There is something heartwarming about this story, especially as it appears not to have been a media stunt ... I have seen no mention of it in the papers. Not that we get many out here, mind you.

10th December 2011: In by Six, Clueless by Seven

As you can imagine, we get a lot of emails, which seek information, give direction or serve to inform. Said messages are often concluded by some stirring strapline under the signature block.

Some of the more common are: "One team, one fight"; "Nothing cannot be solved by hard work"; "We are Log Nation"; and "Shona ba Shona".

My reader in the Green Man will, of course, recognise "Shona ba Shona" as the Dari translation of "Shoulder to Shoulder". These are but a few examples of the many motivational phrases, which I suppose, are designed to encourage us to ever-higher levels of excellence. Of course, they are so customary that in the main, they go unread or rather unnoticed.

Naturally, this has been a source of amusement to me, and I have been sending out a few of my own: "Excellence by breakfast – miracles by dinner"; "We've finished it before you have even thought of it".

But my favourite is "In by six, clueless by seven". My inspiration for that particular quote comes from the folks at home mustering in the Green Man on a Friday evening. I know at least someone who has cottoned on to my discreet witticisms, but I might just remain undiscovered until I get home.

11th December 2011: High Flyer with Experience of Alien Landscapes

It appears that my efforts to secure a job for the Dutchman through assisting with his applications have come to the square root of naff all. Despite job offers from the EU, NATO and contractors that include fat salaries, improved living conditions and ample leave, he has turned them all down.

The prospect of remaining in Afghanistan proved too much, and frankly, who can blame him. The other reason, of course, is that he now wants to be a hotelier, and yours truly has been helping him put his business plan together, although I didn't touch the costings. If it goes well, he and his other half will be making their fortune in the Swedish tourist industry.

It's now in the hands of the bank. I have also been approached by a young American lady who has asked if I could support her future job application. She's a feisty individual, which prompted me to bestow upon her the nickname "Boudicca". She seems quite taken with that, and the name seems to have stuck. If anybody can advise me on how to write a reference for somebody who wants to join the NASA Astronaut Corps, then please get in touch. Something

346

along the lines of high-flyer with experience of alien landscapes, methinks.

12th December 2011: They Don't Have Health Insurance Only Graveyards

The car slowed as the traffic built, and we came to a gentle halt. Adjacent to us was an Afghan cemetery, which stretched up into the hillside. Some graves were covered in a canopy, while others were marked by sun-bleached flags partly attached to spindly sticks, which bent in the wind.

The headstones were formed in irregular rows, which jutted like broken teeth from the dust and sand. These stones were of a similar colour to the earth and the whole blended in as one. A few trucks were parked laden with stone and the drivers squatted by their vehicles. They were either lying over on route to a building site or making provisions for the winter.

The winter will be harsh, which no doubt will mean work for the masons and gravediggers. Who says the Afghans do not plan ahead? I suppose they have to. As the Sergeant Major says, they don't have health insurance ... only graveyards.

13th December 2011: Bootleg Copies are Available

Being someone who can string a sentence together without relying on crayons, I was asked to write the script for this year's panto. This I did, and being a cautious fellow, sent it off to legal for a once over.

The response was considerate, polite and given in such a way so as not to dampen initiative and stifle any future creativity. I can, however, sum the response up in fairly short order: "Not a hope!"

It appears that my literary innovation managed to insult every nationality, command formation and individual lifestyle known to man. I thought it was a complex plot, although I do accept it did rely on a level of tolerance, which was perhaps rather ambitious.

I am aware that legal has sent a copy to High Command for what I suppose will be a final ruling. On being told this, I did ask that my name be omitted from the bottom of the script. This may have been a belated career-saving effort, but there is no need to add to one's vocational demise unnecessarily. I did confide in a mate that I think my script will be blackballed:

"Oh no, it won't," came the reply ... very funny.

Bootleg copies are available pursuant to private correspondence. For the Mursley Players, I do have in mind a cast list and can think of at least one gentleman who would look good in green tights.

14th December 2011: Adds to the Distress

The post room is awash with letters and parcels destined for the troops out here. I have been a beneficiary of this Christian largesse and was seen struggling with a pile of presents that are now sitting comfortably under my scratcher.

Our gallant NCO, the "postie", is working like an elf trying to process this vast quantity of goodies, which seem daily to flood into his sorting office. The relief on his face is palpable as happy soldiers remove swathes of articles releasing room to cope with this steady stream.

The good boys and girls will leave their gifts unopened until Christmas day. The naughty boys and girls, however, will open them on receipt. Such will be their excitement. It may, of course, be because they are a little wiser. It only adds to the distress of loved ones when the Army has to return its dead's unopened presents as well as other personal effects.

15th December 2011: Happy Holidays

Once a week, we muster to remember those who have lost their lives over the previous week. Each nation has a representative who calls the roll of those from his or her military who has died. I do not know why but we do not read the honour roll of those Afghans who are killed, but if we did, I suspect we would be there a lot longer.

The Chaplain oversees the event, which is a ceremony rather than a service. A "ceremony", it seems, is more accommodating of the coalition environment rather than "service". A "service" would apply to a particular faith, whereas a "ceremony" would not. It also appears that soldiers can be ordered to attend a "ceremony" but not a "service".

Therefore, the Chaplain has to be on his guard in order to ensure that prayers do not invoke Jesus Christ or any other religious figure for that matter but rather reflect some higher being. I'm sure my Muslim mate wouldn't be bothered either way and would still show up out of respect for his colleagues. This avoidance of faith is in direct contrast to what goes on in the place of work.

I've practically tripped over bibles and Christian icons. Indeed, of my team of four, three of us are churchgoers, and the fourth I'd suggest is a supporter rather than a participant. This then leads me to the subject of "happy holidays", which is a ghastly American term aimed at complying with their constitution or something. In the public areas, all traditional Christmas decorations appear stripped of any Christian imagery, and yet in the offices, it's different. I'm just waiting for somebody to wish me "happy holiday" when I'll politely remind them that I "aint on no holiday" but will, of course, wish them a Merry Christmas. And just for the record, if it's God's wish that I cop it out here, I want a Christian military funeral with all the trimmings, and notwithstanding the reverence in which it is undertaken I do not want any mumbo jumbo half-cocked "ceremony".

Also, I do not care if it rains as it will not bother me. Gosh, I'm in a stroppy mood today.

16h December 2011: The Consumption of Booze

The metal barrier lying obliquely across the road gave me the impression that perhaps something had happened. It appears that I have been operating under a misunderstanding.

Despite my inability to encounter a drop of the hard stuff, others appear to have had far less difficulty. The newly created obstruction was the consequence of some booze being in the driver who was in the car that was in the barrier. However, the car had long since gone, but I'll wager the fall out will not be. High Command had recently ordered us all to re-read the driving directive.

This was because the number of road traffic accidents causing injury to civilians was not helping our cause. Obeying speed limits was one such measure High Command has insisted on. I noticed one Afghan road sign in English that either read 20.25 Kilometres Per Hour or 20-25 KPH. Either way, it impressed me. The consumption of booze may also explain the loud noises emanating from the office of a very senior gentleman.

It was quite clear to those passing that some chap was being given an absolute rifting. The nationality of the gentleman concerned suggests it may be related to the discovery by an American soldier of one sozzled individual who'd fallen from the second floor of a stairwell while his mucker laid comatose in an adjacent room. They being countrymen of the said senior gentleman, had us putting two and two together and making four. Clearly, the proximity of Christmas is having an adverse influence on peoples' judgment.

Still, there'll be no Christmas tipple for me. Indeed, we don't get so much as a good night kiss out here. Well, I don't at any rate and nor do those with whom I work. Although I can't speak for everybody ...

17th December 2011: Paraplegic Olympics

Presumably, because I can use cutlery and readily identify the appropriate side plate, I was dragooned into a party of officers constituted to have lunch with a very important General indeed. He was visiting the Theatre from more comfortable quarters in order to improve his situational awareness.

We had soup to start with, so I was conscious not to slurp. The conversation was lively. All is not well in other Theatres, and there is much with which to be concerned. The subject matter turned to the Olympics, and we were counselled not to take leave during this period. It seems that those responsible have badly miscalculated, and the Armed Forces will now need to be used in considerable numbers to ensure that this overpriced al-Qaida magnet goes well.

The conversation turned to the sporting events and whether folk had tickets or not. My initial grasp of the discussion suggested that the ticket lottery had, for reasons unknown, favoured those in khaki. It soon became clear that this was not the case as the events being referred to involve the Paraplegic Olympics.

Thanks to Iraq and Afghanistan, a number of the athletes are former military personnel. It was their success that was of import to those quaffing a medley of culinary offerings. The success or otherwise of Lycra encased apprentice millionaires seemed to arouse no interest at all.

18th December 2011: Heavy Jowls Danced on His Chin

I watched, fascinated at the smooth rhythmic strokes that is Dari gliding effortlessly across the page. His chubby fingers lightly gripped the tortoiseshell fountain pen as he jotted down the remarks made by the interpreter. It was an important meeting, and I sat along the wall too junior for a seat at the table.

The Dari author suddenly looked up. His heavy jowls danced on his chin as he summarily dismissed the "Terp" with a few words and a wave of his hand. The lad looked crestfallen. Momentarily lost and embarrassed, he was shuffled out by another who was instantly appointed by the man with the pen. I leant forward from my chair.

"Over here, son, come and sit by me."

The lad did so, trying to mumble an apology. There are twelve who live in his home; he needs the job. I told him not to worry but who will look after him when we are gone?

The tortoiseshell pen seemed to accelerate in its exertions. I was fascinated by the pen. It looked expensive. I spoke later. So are his Armani suits and the Mercedes cars for his sons. You obviously do well out here on a public salary and perhaps another revenue stream. It's a good use of our taxpayer's money, I'm sure. Otherwise, we would only waste it on things like daycare for the elderly.

Later I fixed it for our "Terp" to translate on behalf of our General in front of an audience of 200, which included some even more important people. He nailed it.

19th December 2011: If Not Enough were Killed

I bimbled across the base. I'd successfully extricated myself from the office at a comfortable 2030. My mobile rings.

"Sir, the British Brigadier is looking for you."

"Strap back, Sergeant Major; I've only just got away."

"Hello, would you mind awfully popping in, I've a guest I need looking after while I attend to a couple of things."

"Give me two minutes, sir, and I'll be there."

Clearly, the Brigadier was now in possession of the cell phone. We'd served together in Northern Ireland. He'd spent his career saving the lives of our precious boys and girls, and now he was trying to do the same for the Afghans. Such is my respect for him. I was happy to help. That said, I also know an order when I hear one.

I polled up in a timely fashion and was introduced in haste to a lady who seemed somewhat familiar. She was, in fact, a BBC news reporter who is a household name. Blimey, I thought, I've got to up my game here, so I took her across to the recreational centre for a hot chocolate and a chat. She was extremely confident, obviously articulate and had an urgent intelligence.

Qualities no doubt from having a diplomat father, a private education and a university degree underpinned by a more than passing acquaintance with the Notting Hill set. Matched against her was yours truly of unknown parentage, a secondary school education and a polytechnic degree underpinned by a more than passing acquaintance with the Green Man set.

I, therefore, needed to play to my strengths. To that end, I knocked her bandy with some of my best jokes and a few ditties about army life. She did grimace at one point, though, that may be because some soldiers in the background were slaughtering a karaoke version of "I've got a feeling" by the Black Eyed Peas. The Brigadier soon arrived and perhaps rescued us both.

Somewhat earlier, the Taliban had attacked a police station. Her news desk was tracking the event, and she was standing by, ready to respond to her Blackberry. It appeared that the criterion for her being deployed to cover the story was the number of deaths and injuries. The conclusion I made was that if not enough were killed, she wouldn't be tasked, and therefore, the Taliban wouldn't get the publicity they desire.

Even someone like me with the IQ of a poorly educated Neanderthal could work out that there was something unpleasant in what this implied. The BBC will only cover a story if there is a suitable volume of death and mutilation. Therefore, the Taliban will not get the media profile they want unless they provide it.

The deduction is extremely disconcerting, especially as I know where she will be going for Christmas. I do hope the Taliban don't save her any bother by delivering a story to her doorstep.

20th December 2011: More Deserving Than Others

Well, I've been given another medal for services to NATO. It comes with the rations, and everybody cops for one who has served in ISAF. We were paraded in four rows in front of four Generals, who each walked down a line presenting medals.

Each general was followed by a Macedonian holding a huge tray resplendent with twinkling metal discs. Whilst I've been awarded this ISAF medal, British military regulations do not permit me to wear it. It seems I will also be given an Op HERRICK medal, and one cannot wear two medals for the same campaign. It does seem ironic, though, that the only medal I have ever been formally presented with should be the only medal I'm not authorised to wear.

The other huge irony is that it was a French General who presented it to me, a proud Englishman. He struggled to pin it on my combat jacket as the thick material caused some problems. I suggested that my manly chest may be the source of the difficulty, and whilst this created titters in the ranks, it didn't make it any easier.

Somebody once said that the number of medals on a man's chest is inversely proportional to his distance from the front line. I think I now understand why that would be the case. If you are on the front line, the chances of having another medal are reduced by death or injury.

Moreover, the experiences are such that if you get away unscathed, you may not want to hang around in the Army for another one. We all deserve our medals, but some of us are more deserving than others. Or, to put it more bluntly, a one-legged soldier with one medal trumps, a two-legged soldier with six.

21st December 2011: Thumb up Bum and Mind in Neutral

As soldiers, it is drilled into us to be situationally aware. Look at what is around you. What has changed? Why has it changed? Number four Sligo Avenue always has three pints of milk a day. Why are there six? Are there guests? Who are these guests? Why are they here?

The absence of the normal is the presence of the abnormal. Is something out of place? If so, why is this? Are the people behaving as normal? Look around you, stay focussed and concentrate. Look up, look down, look around, look forward, look back. Listen. Use your senses. If it doesn't look right, it isn't right. Do all this and keep you and your mates alive.

So how in the heck did a soldier bimble across a strip of 100 metres of freshly laid concrete in broad daylight surrounded by Afghans with spades? Just in case he was short-sighted, there was a cement mixer making a noise like a washing machine full of bricks.

Figuratively speaking, "thumb up bum and mind in neutral" seems the likely cause. If he'd have been British, I would have had a sense of humour failure. As he wasn't, I made a mental note not to go out on the ground with him.

22nd December 2011: There Will Be No Thank You Letters

I'm freezing my pods off out here. It's as hot as Iraq is in the summer and as cold as northern Norway is in the winter. What a climate. It's cold and dry. The Pakistanis tell me that it's not good for your health.

This is because the dust is alive with toxins, and being cold and dry, there is no rain to wash it out of the atmosphere. This might explain why my cellmate has been ill for the last few days, and you can hear the coughing of others during the night. In the morning, there is smog from all the fires the Afghans have lit to keep warm. They appear to burn anything they can get their hands on. This need comes on top of the many workshops that manufacture all sorts of things while gaily pumping out the attendant pollutants.

At night I seldom see any stars, which I think, is because the mountains trap a cloud of gunk over the place, which blocks out the twinkling. All in all, it's like early 20th century London. It cannot be good for your health, and those out running in the morning are sucking in lungfuls of the stuff. Still, I've no complaints. Five Polish lads killed today in a single IED strike made sure of that. They would, I suspect, have received their Christmas presents by now. There will be no thank you letters.

23rd December 2011: When the Soul Feels Pain

"Oh Lord, we are wearing body armour, but please grant us your armour as we ask for protection ..."

Yours truly was having second thoughts about going on this particular trip after the team leader had called us together for a pre-deployment prayer. I'm a big fan of prayer, but timing is everything, and I'm not keen if it is going to scare me.

The Church group to which I belong was off to an orphanage to issue some much-needed blankets and supplies to the children. The leader of this Christian gaggle obviously felt the need to pray prior to mounting our vehicles. The Lieutenant with responsibility for the vehicle packet obviously felt the need to brief us about the IED threat and actions on contact. Couldn't we just post the supplies, I thought?

The trip took about 30 minutes as we laboured through the city, and yes, I did notice the wrong turning.

On arrival, we debussed and were promptly swamped by a number of children who had an excellent grasp of the English word "chocolate". The little mites were very grubby (reminded me of myself at their age) but were nevertheless cheerful. But this was more than just an orphanage.

It was also the headquarters of the Afghan Scout movement and provided a women's refuge. Being a lad with an appetite, I ended up in what I suppose was the bakery. It was a ruined building of two rooms, one of which was full of rubbish. The other wasn't much better, but it did have a hole in the ground, which was the oven. Two women were baking unleavened bread, and rows of neat round dough balls were laid on linen with a damp sheet over them. You needed the linen. The floor was filthy, and this dirt base was where all the food preparation was done.

There were no tables, just bowls for mixing and piles of firewood. A woman working cross-legged with bare feet flattened the dough onto a cushion, which she then used to slap the dough onto the side of the oven. Leaning forward as she did so, her veil slipped from her shoulders. The dough cooked within a couple of minutes, and then she nimbly pulled it off with her fingers. Jesus would have recognised the scene.

Also, under a sheet was a small pile of goodies that a little lad had stashed. If he was trying to hide it, he'd failed miserably. I'm assuming the women were from the refuge and that their role was to look after the orphans. I did see an elderly gentleman who seemed familiar with the place. His crutches sank into the sand as his single leg swung with his movements.

I looked at the Sergeant Major, who seemed very satisfied. He considered the place OK as he hadn't been moved to tears. I, however, couldn't make that claim. It's a strange sensation when the soul feels pain.

24th December 2011: You Can't Say the Head Chef Hasn't Got a Sense of Humour

Do you know what I really miss? Yes ... a cheese board. They do not have such a thing in our cookhouse, which is most un-officer like. My longing for Fromage gave me cause to fill out one of those customer satisfaction chits that were parked strategically by the exits.

This I did and asked if it would be possible to have some Stilton. Well, I never. Said item was on the servery within the week. There was only one drawback. They served it at breakfast as they did my other little fancy; olives. You can't say the head chef hasn't got a sense of humour. He reminds us all of this on the rare occasion that we have fried eggs.

They resemble a dismembered cowpat, which could explain why the Army slang for a cook is "slop jockey". The Christmas menu has been extensively advertised and is to include goose. No doubt we'll get that for breakfast as well.

One Box Per Soldier

Our Christmas boxes have arrived. One box per soldier serving on operations. They contain a range of what are quality goodies and are organised by a charity called uk4u. Other stuff is pouring in. The Chapel is positively bursting with chocolate, sweets and toiletries. We'll all smell lovely tomorrow.

Book of Numbers

The Royal Air Force C of E Chaplain will not make it to see us on Christmas Day, but an American will. Our chaplain has a large parish, which includes the British Embassy.

The C of E Chaplain has already organised a carol service for the troops, and to make it entertaining for them, included a "carol-oke". He put across the story of the birth of Jesus in the form of a quiz, which also included general knowledge and sport. As he dashes about in an armoured vehicle dispensing the Christian message, he must look back in wonder at his previous career as an accountant.

Still, he's probably on good terms with the Old Testament's Book of Numbers. Get it? Oh, please yourself.

25th December 2011: The Problem with Pain

We paraded at the appointed time for the weekly memorial ceremony. The roll call of the dead was read out by a representative from the country that had endured the loss. On Christmas Eve, an RAF lad was added to the list.

Killed this week were five Poles, two Brits, one American and 14 Afghans. To add to their woes, a coal mine had collapsed, killing 13 miners. The thoughts of us soldiers were with the families of those who had lost loved ones. Being Christmas, it made the occasion particularly solemn. The problem with pain is you cannot lighten its load through sharing.

At the end of the ceremony, we were dismissed and went off to work. Late last night, our Dutch General had left a gift on the desk of each one of his staff. With the gift was a printed note, which he had personalised with a manuscript comment.

It was a superb gesture and hugely appreciated.

The roll call, however, had taken the edge off the day.

"Happy Christmas, Jack."

"Is it?"

Later I turned on my iPod. "Heaven Can Wait" by Meatloaf. Remind me to delete that track.

26th December 2011: A Nice Touch

I'm down by the head with Christmas gifts. Not since I was a desirable bachelor have I been indulged with so many presents. It took me an hour to open them all. And what an eclectic mix they were.

One reader clearly felt the need to send an air freshener, which went down well with the lads. Why I have no idea, however, this was more than offset by the panic caused by my receiving a Christmas card adorned with Brussel sprouts.

The Russian doll was a novel gift, as were the reindeer hats, a box of Lego, yoyos and a flashing bow tie. All these gifts have rather undermined my reputation for being a serious player out here. The shortbread, Christmas cake and mince pies were superb, the watch excellent, and the books much appreciated.

The Kit Kat, carefully concealed in a much-needed pair of socks, was a nice touch. I received several bags of chocolate coins. One of which were Euros. Like the real thing, I suspect they won't last very long. All these gifts were underpinned by an email account glowing with Christmas cards and Christmas good wishes.

Sincerest thanks and gratitude from me and the gannets who are now looking enviously at my box of chocolate chunk cookies.

27th December 2011: School Books are Very Expensive Out Here

My colleague arrived at the forward operating base and was met by a number of British lads who included a handsome young officer, all hair and a physique like a surfer.

Resembling something from Hollywood Central casting, he was not only physically blessed but also radiated charm. My colleague was briefed that tomorrow this young officer would be taking much-needed supplies to a local school with the interpreter and some of our lads. The "Terp" had been in Theatre for a month, having completed eighteen months at the Defence School of Languages.

The bloke he'd taken over from had raised money to buy gear for the school. All they had to do was close the loop on this charitable enterprise and deliver the goods. The project all sounded very exciting, so much so that my oppo thought about going along with them. He decided not to.

After all, he was quite senior to them and didn't want to steal their thunder. Moreover, he was sure that if he asked, they would readily agree, but in their hearts, he knew that they wouldn't want to be burdened by an old fat knacker. Ten hours later, the young officer was dead, the Terp very seriously injured, and the lads hurt. They'd hit a landmine. On Christmas Eve, the Terp died of his wounds.

School books are very expensive out here, especially it seems at Christmas.

28th December 2011: Assumption is the Mother of Cockup

It was quite an important meeting, and I'd gone to a lot of trouble to ensure that all was in place. After all ... planning and preparation prevent p**s poor performance. Moreover, he who fails to plan, plans to fail. Yours truly was covering all eventualities so much so that I even had the slides translated into Dari, so our Afghan colleagues could follow events.

During the meeting, an Afghan General leaned across and whispered to my General that there was an error in the English to Dari translation. The General gave me a look as if to say:

"What the f**k over?"

I responded to the effect of how the heck was I to know if there had been an error. Despite my brilliance in most things, a comprehensive understanding of Dari grammar was not one of them. The slides frankly could have said anything, and I would have been absolutely none the wiser.

Besides, as the work had been done by the Afghans in the translation office, I had assumed that they might just have a Scoobie (clue) as to what they were doing.

Once I had made my point, albeit far more tactfully than I have documented, the General gave an amused smile. This suggested that he had understood my predicament entirely. Nothing was said on the subject again.

There had, however, been a failure on my watch. As a young officer, I recollect being told that I was responsible for every aspect of my mission. Whether or not I was to blame for any failing was a matter for others to decide. I'll not be caught out again.

I shall get another Afghan to proofread any future translations. Mind you, the whole experience was further confirmation of that old adage that "assumption" is the mother of "cock-up".

29th December 2011: A Language All of Their Own

All in all, there are one or two things that have made this tour less miserable than it otherwise could have been. One of which is knocking around with soldiers again.

That said, they have a language all of their own, and sometimes I'm at a loss as to what they are talking about. Take, for example, a cup of tea. A young Lieutenant was taking tea orders from her lads. One fellow asked for a Julie Andrews, and another wanted a Whoopie Goldberg. I know what a NATO standard is, namely a white tea with two sugars.

It appears a Julie Andrews is a white none (Nun), and a Whoopie Goldberg is a black none (Nun). I went for a Julie. Had I asked for a Kylie Minogue, I'd have got a white with one lump. Of course, there are also the nicknames that soldiers give to one another. If you are from Scotland, then obviously expect to be called "Jock" and if you are from Liverpool "Scouse". The influence of a surname may take priority, and if you are called "Ellis," then you may be addressed as "Siph".

Methinks She Doth Protest Too Much

What I would say about our soldiers, and I do so with a great deal of pride, is that I have never heard a single derogatory remark made about the Afghans. That said, I have heard plenty of disparaging remarks made about the other nationalities with which we share this base.

I also encountered a young British soldier being given a thoroughly colourful dressing down by a foreign lady who had an excellent command of Anglo-Saxon expletives. It appears the lad had been very considerate and offered to wipe a mark off the girl's forehead. There was, in fact, no mark on her forehead. She then proceeded to walk across the base with a huge black smear.

It was for this crime that he was being admonished. The attendant theatricals required her to take her sunglasses off. She then placed them on a table where another soldier took advantage of the distraction and used them to engineer a further misfortune. At this stage, I thinned out quickly. My command of the Manual of Military Law didn't equip me to intercede, and moreover, I assessed the situation as young people having fun. Methinks the girl doth protest too much and was enjoying the attention.

30th December 2011: Purple Heart

I seem to have a fan. Apparently, it's my accent that attracts her. It makes her feel comfortable. Well, it's hardly my looks, is it? She frequently drops into the office to say hello. A Jamaican girl, she spent six years living in England but subsequently joined the US Army.

She's a civilian now working on some project. She sports a very unmilitary hairstyle and dresses in the style of a young American. She certainly likes to talk a lot. It's a shame, I suppose, that I'm not the garrulous type. She's also found common ground with the Sergeant Major, whose wife's family has Caribbean and English relatives.

"She wasn't in the Army long, Sergeant Major ... what two years?" I mused after a particularly long conversation.

"Her career ended abruptly with a Purple Heart, a dead friend beside her and a medical discharge," came the reply.

That statement certainly killed the conversation.

31st December 2011: Please Stop Singing Along to Your iPod

The lad started hopping from one foot to the next, a sure sign that he was unsure as to what to do. He'd loaded his bread onto one of those toasters that grills the slice as it is carried over a heating element by a conveyor.

His problem was that all the bread had not been retrieved, and a light plume of smoke was forming over the toaster. He put his hand in and then whipped it out, and then jumped behind the instrument to try and unplug it.

By this stage, he'd caught the attention of about 300 diners who were gradually falling into silence as the plume evolved into a violent projection of smoke in the manner of steam belching from a locomotive's whistle.

You could sense his embarrassment as he tried desperately to quell the smoke. The assembled mass was now gawping at him, and when the expected happened, there was an outburst of applause. He'd set the fire alarm off. The noise was excruciating the situation, however safe. A colleague nudged me to complain about the noise.

"Yes, it is nasty; the fire alarm is designed to encourage people to evacuate," I explained over the noise.

"It's not that. Can you please stop singing along to your iPod?"

January 2012

Tommy

I went into an M-O-B a looking for some fuel,

The contractor 'e up's an sez, "I've ten days less for you."

The staff be'ind the HQ they coughed an' choked to die,

I outs to my computer to write a new reply:

O it's Tommy this, an' Tommy that an' contractor, "Where's my fuel?"

"Well it's stuck behind the Khyber Pass but we're moving it to you."

It's stuck behind the Khyber Pass o what a thing to do?

The loggie knows he has to trust and pay your invoice too.

Yes, makin' mock o' contractors that charge you while you sleep;

Is Cheaper than them Tommies, an they're prison cheap;

An' sacking honest Tommies when they cost a little more,

Is five times better business than seeing shares on the floor.

Then it's Tommy this, an' Tommy that, an "Tommy, where's yer scoff?"

"It's stuck behind the Khyber Pass with all our other stuff."

"Tell me not you've contracted out the delivery of your supplies?"

"Oh yes we did it'll be alright so long as nobody dies."

With Apologies To Rudyard Kipling

DISCLAIMER: The author disassociates himself from any suggestion that this is a criticism of policy. The content is simply an amusing aside for the purposes of entertainment only and should not in any way be construed as a comment on Defence contracting policy.

1st January 2012: Poor Documentation

The Padre was bereft of his replacement at this morning's service. As a consequence, he'd been told to "stag on". His successor had had a problem at Brize Norton. When his documents were checked prior to his flight, it was discovered he had an out of date ID card ... oh, that old trick!

The funny thing, though, is that poor documentation is not unique to us Brits. We were advised that a German General was having trouble with his travel arrangements due to the date having elapsed on his passport. Well, of course, this was manna from heaven to me.

Once I'd got over the shock of learning that a German's papers were not in order, I felt obliged to comment. I thus remarked that I thought as a race they weren't overly concerned with such matters as border control. After all, it had not bothered them in the past, so why should it be an issue now?

I'd chosen my audience well, although my German paratrooper friend gave me a look as if to say I was trying his patience. Sometimes I just can't help myself. It's a wonder I'm still in a job.

2nd January 2012: Should the Taste of Our Female Readers Change

Dear Sir,

Thank you for your recent submission for consideration in our next edition of Playgirl. Unfortunately, on this occasion, we do not feel able to publish your photographs. However, should the taste of our female readers change, we may be able to accommodate them in the future. Without wishing to intrude on private grief, our photographic editor was wondering if you'd ever been shot or grew up riding a bike awkwardly?

Yours sincerely,

Editor Playgirl magazine

A colleague received the above letter with the appropriate letterhead and logos, albeit he wasn't serving in Afghanistan at the time. He was the victim of a spoof and had been set up by his colleagues. Although the incident is not related to this Theatre, the story did nevertheless bring a few much-needed laughs.

3rd January 2012: Only the Manufacturer's Opinion

Everybody out here has an iPod. I was the exception to this rule until home on leave when I bought one for my 50th birthday. My iPod and I are now inseparable, so you can understand why I went into shock when it wouldn't work. Being a Luddite, I sought advice.

A new charger was used, various Dutchmen had a go. I was then referred to a colleague who has a detailed understanding of all things iPod. He explained how they were manufactured, what parts were mechanical and what electronic. The upshot of all this technical advice was that none of us could restore it to a working condition.

I resigned myself to being iPod less for the remainder of my tour. Indeed, one of the unwritten rules is that when your iPod packs up, it is time to go home. That mine had chosen to do so with a week to run added to my frustration.

Finally, I had no choice but to consult the manual. I fixed it within four minutes. Well, what do they know? It's only the manufacturer's opinion, after all.

4th January 2012: Social Mobility Based on Hard Work

I liked the bloke within 60 seconds of meeting him. We seemed to see eye to eye on everything. Well: we are the same height. What is more, we'd both spent time at sea, so we had a shared appreciation of matters nautical.

His experiences, however, were somewhat different to mine. He'd gone to sea to escape the tyranny of the communist takeover of Vietnam. His mum was Chinese, and his dad Vietnamese. They were to be reassigned from the city to work the land. As a consequence, a group of them got together, found the money and fled.

I asked him about the voyage to Malaysia, where they had landed. I wanted to know about the boat, the conditions and how the trip was undertaken. He told me that he was eight years old at the time and that it was all just one big adventure. I'd read about the Vietnamese boat people and what had happened to some of them at the hands of pirates. It was horrific, so I didn't press my curiosity. He did say he liked the refugee camp as he didn't have to go to school.

Strange isn't it that a foster kid and a Vietnamese boat person should find themselves over three decades later teaming up to try and help the Afghans. Clearly, his lack of education at the refugee camp had no lasting adverse effects. He was definitely the custodian of this particular duo's brain cell. He is, after all, a doctor who had considered becoming a dentist.

They must have good schools in America, which is where he and his family fetched up. He's also a US Army Lieutenant Colonel. Social mobility based on hard work, opportunity and application. I liked him, and the people of the USA should feel very proud of their culture, which allowed him to reach his potential.

5th January 2012: Queuing up to Leave

We Brits were a bit out of sorts this morning on learning that one of our lads, after 18 months at the military hospital in Birmingham, had succumbed to his wounds. Eighteen months of fight. But you would expect nothing less of a Gurkha.

How his family is coping, I have no idea. The laughing Dutchman shared our pain. He is especially sensitive to mutilations. It bothers him, and he has mentioned it on more than one occasion. The sense of loss was heightened when somebody made a pointed remark. It seems that articulate, intelligent and educated able boded Afghans of military age are queuing up to leave the country and make new lives for themselves in America.

I have some very forthright views concerning that observation. We have teenagers fighting and dying to improve the lot of their countrymen. They meanwhile are legging it while those Afghans of lesser means are stepping up to the plate. It's perhaps best if I said nothing further.

Good Advice

A US National Guardsman, who is a lawyer by trade, described being here as like living in an open prison. He had, however, learnt from his "customers" in the penitentiary some tricks and tips as to how to handle it. On average, they were serving over 20 years each, so he must have had some exceedingly good advice.

Splashes of Red

A very senior British general described our lives working and living in Afghanistan as being grey. I don't mind grey. I can do grey. It's the splashes of red that really bother me.

6th January 2012: I Liken It to Playing Baseball

Days to do are getting few, but my approach to work is like my approach to playing rugby. You only stop when someone blows a whistle or taps you on the shoulder to tell you that you have been substituted.

I have heard no whistle and felt no tap, so I'll continue to drive on until I board the transport home. At the moment, I'm trying to get a briefing paper in front of the top man. Before it arrives on his desk, it has to be staffed between three Generals of equivalent rank and then go through two more of increasing seniority. I liken it to playing baseball.

The ultimate boss is fourth base. At first base is the three Generals of equivalent rank, second base is a German General, third base is a French General and then voila! I've struck the paper four times now. The first strike got all the way to the outer office of fourth base, and then some functionary wanted the format of the paper changed, so back it came.

My second strike reached the French General, but he was unhappy, so it came tumbling back down again. This was because in order to successfully navigate it through first base, I'd so sanitised the content it was, I must agree,

397

somewhat bland. My third strike didn't even make it past second base, and it was sent straight back for further tweaking. I'm now on my fourth strike.

Interestingly this is a markedly different approach to that adopted by a Polish General. He door stopped me on an issue and invited me to comment there and then. This I did and proceeded to download the problem and what needed to be done about it. This technique has no "gate guard" filtering what is and what isn't said and therefore enjoys the merit of speed, honesty, economy of effort and efficiency.

On a personal note, it also enjoys the advantage of there being no written record to adversely affect your annual report should you have documented a view that your boss wasn't happy with. That's why good officers command by walking about, meeting soldiers and finding out first-hand what is going on; rather than sitting back and being told what their staff want them to hear.

This is why I recently stood to attention and briefed on my feet when a German General walked in and enquired as to my activities.

7th January 2012: Which Would You Prefer?

The vehicle packet rumbled into our location and came to a halt. Soldiers jumped out and then proceeded to guide their transport back into the parking bays. They were dressed for war, looked efficient and went about their business with purpose. They were, after all, our lot. I'd expect nothing less.

Once they were in position, the rear doors were swung open, and they started climbing out to go about their business. It had been a simple admin move, and having arrived safely, the troops took on a more relaxed demeanour. A soldier riding top cover took off her helmet and goggles and then placed them on the roof of the vehicle.

Removing a hair clip, she shook her head in the way that girls do, which caused her auburn locks to tumble gracefully down over her shoulders. I stood there completely transfixed, having expected to see some hairy arsed soldier. What I was looking at was a girl who looked no older than my eldest daughter pausing in the sunlight having just ridden shotgun. She had a mature beauty about her, a consequence of nature rather than makeup tips.

Her parents would have been extraordinarily proud of her had they seen this feminine beauty emerging like a butterfly from the harsh rigours of soldiering. I walked on as our troops reverted to the youngsters that they are, laughing and bounding up the stairs to see the Sergeant. She had ridden top cover. The last time I had spoken on the subject was to a young soldier carrying out that role as we drove through the city.

As his head and shoulders stood proud of the vehicle, he told me of his fear of being decapitated by an IED. I spoke to another whose fear on riding in the back was that an IED would leave him trapped and burning to death. Which would you prefer? Stuck in the back and burning to death or riding top cover and being decapitated?

8th January 2012: The Mud and the Blood

I'm sat here counting my ammunition prior to my departure. Her Majesty would take a very dim view were I to have lost any. I know where I need to be to start my trip home because a chap phoned me about a certain appointment so as to confuse anybody who was listening in. As I squeeze everything into my bags, I liken it to returning from holiday when you wonder why you seem to have so much more kit than when you arrived.

Last night we said our farewells. I told some hopeless jokes and made a little speech. It is quite emotional leaving behind those who are staying on, but as I said to the General, I'd be considerably more emotional were he to order me to stay. For me, this tour will not end until I know that my team are all safely home. Unlike that poor infantry soldier who took his own life this week.

The death of his two friends saw that his tour would never end, and it appears he could no longer live with it. I note that one of his dead muckers was of Middle Eastern heritage, which suggests that neither race, religion or culture is a barrier to the love of one British soldier for another.

I can assure my reader in the Green Man that there is none of that racist nonsense out here. There are just two colours; the mud and the blood; which is a quote I borrowed from General Colin Powell, the best President America didn't have.

As I hand myself into the safe care of the RAF, I have, of course, configured myself emotionally for the experience. Crab Air is seldom pleasant. Before I do so, however, I will attend the weekly memorial ceremony. I owe those who didn't make it at least that much.

9th January 2012: Extremely Jack Thing to Do

My journey began with a security brief before we mounted our vehicles. It went along the lines of the enemy has got ABC, and they intend to do XYZ, and if they do, we will carry out the following. I thought that walking might be a preferable option.

When I arrived at the first stage of the journey, things were looking up. The Sergeant who met me I'd served with before, and he advised me to catch the flight tonight and then slipped me the key to the VIP room, so I could have a nap. When I say VIP, I mean "Army VIP" which is a considerably different standard to what my reader in the Green Man would be accustomed to.

I think it was the ironing board that upgraded it to "VIP" status. Still, it was quiet, and I had no complaints. At dark o'clock, we flew out and arrived at a main operating base at 00:30. It was at this juncture that things started to unravel.

Once I and three others had cleared the flight line, we discovered that those who'd got to the transport first set off without us. Apart from being an extremely jack thing to do, it was also exceptionally brave. One of us four amigos was a shaven-headed commando with an interesting facial scar. I figured immediately that should we catch up with those who'd left us behind, I would be in for some entertainment. He was a Half Colonel. The other chap was a cavalry Major, and the fourth chap was a soldier from the Intelligence Corps. After 30 minutes, the contracted transport arrived, and we all hopped in, encouraged by the cold.

After a "not my job, I'm airframes" conversation in pidgin English, we hopped off again. There was no way this driver was going to take us to where we needed to be. The next bus to arrive looked as if it had been re-commissioned from former employment as a hen house, but what the heck, we boarded never the less.

The driver was a Bosnian who was over here for two years, working 13 hours a day for a take-home salary of $43K per annum tax-free. He dropped us off at the British enclave on what is a huge base that makes Heathrow look like a gliding club. We jumped off the bus, tired and emotional, looking for the transit accommodation. It was the wrong bl**dy enclave!

We had no idea where we were. At this stage, I realised why our ammunition had been taken from us as I was about ready to shoot someone. The young soldier I could tell was becoming very disappointed in the standard of leadership being shown by two Half Colonels and a Major. After tramping around for a while, we encountered another bus.

There was no negotiation. We jumped on and eventually got to where we needed to be. The driver shuffled us off surreptitiously with the remark that he shouldn't be there. While queuing to book in, I encountered my relief. He looked tired, knackered and disorientated, having just flown in from Blighty. I, therefore, gave him his "in- brief" from 02:00 to 03:30. We had served at sea together in 20 Maritime Regiment RCT.

He will have no problems. I fell onto my cot at about 04:00 and figured I didn't need to set my alarm for breakfast because I was sure any one of the other twelve blokes or, indeed, the aircraft noise would wake me. As expected, we were awoken; five minutes after the cookhouse closed. This may have proved too much for the Commando. I think he went off looking for somebody.

10th January 2012: Principles of Communal Living

Splendid fellows though they are our police friends have absolutely no idea as to the principles of communal living. A group of them shared our transit accommodation, much to the frustration of the soldiers. There are no Queen's Regulations as such, which govern behaviour, but the following are a few hints.

1. Firstly, do not turn the light on when you get up. You have a torch: use it. Moreover, you should prepare your kit the night before for extraction in darkness. This allows those around you who do not need to get up the opportunity to continue with their kip.

2. Secondly, do not start up a conversation with your mates about what you are going to do that day. It does not help the mission, and the rest of the lads are not remotely interested.

3. Thirdly, the British soldier is used to smells. Turning his living accommodation into the film set of a Sir Henry Cooper TV advert is not appreciated. Use roll-on deodorant. It doesn't stink the place out and make a noise like a compressed fart.

4. Fourthly, if you have ignored rule one, please turn the light off when leaving. This will save a soldier having to ask you to do so.

5. The fifth rule is that when you return to your bed space because you did not prepare your kit properly and have subsequently left something behind, please do not repeat your omission of rule one.

The above can also be viewed as a set of safety precautions should you find that you are, in fact, sharing your accommodation with infantry soldiers fresh from the fight.

This is especially relevant if, during the night, your manhood necessitates your inviting some girls into the tent to show them how to put their body armour together. Feminine discourse may arouse one manly trait and the constant noise of Velcro another. It's best not to arouse sleeping soldiers in either sense. The key to success is letting them sleep.

A Flight Home

My reader in the Green Man will be delighted to learn that I have now secured a seat on a flight home. However, the excitement of buying me a beer in the said hostelry needs to be held in abeyance. There are several stages in the process, which includes an overlay in Cyprus for what they call decompression training. Any one of these stages can be met by further delay. Therefore, it is best not to allow yourself to be disappointed.

In brief, the decompression training involves presentations by a medic and a priest. The medic will naturally be concerned about your physical health, and the priest unsurprisingly will concern himself with emotional and spiritual issues. There is a barbeque laid on and a couple of comedians. The events are underpinned by controlled access to alcohol.

I say controlled because the quantities would come as a considerable disappointment to Mursley's Friday night revellers, who consider it a cultural shortcoming that spirits are not served in pints. Still (no pun intended), this is a very sensible measure (again, no pun intended) considering many of these lads will have come straight from the fight.

This Hit the Medic Really Hard

As it happens, while waiting to check-in, I fell into conversation with a young infantry Lieutenant who was going on R&R with some of his boys. He had the physical appearance of a Victorian officer that you would see in paintings of some great action that adorn the walls of wood-panelled officers' messes.

He was a comprehensive lad who'd read law at a distinguished northern university. He didn't really know why he chose law. This was in direct contrast to another young officer who had read drama at a distinguished West Country university. When I asked him why he said he enjoys drama, and the ratio of girls to boys was much in his favour.

Moreover, the situation was further advantaged by some of the male competition not having the same inclinations. I suppose at least it was an honest response.

The infantry officer gave me a 60-minute master class in the tactical employment of troops on the ground and life in a patrol base. He described getting a rifting from his Commanding Officer for allowing his men to adopt a kitten. Said moggie had scratched one of the soldiers, which necessitated medical treatment back in a main operating base and the temporary loss of a much-needed fighting man from the front line.

The kitten was much admired for its ability to catch mice, especially as one soldier had been bitten by an irate mouse when he inadvertently put his hand on it. This was all low-level conversation and did serve to amuse. That is until he described the death of one of his soldiers and how the medic couldn't go forward because the ground was littered with IEDs.

The lad's mates were able to get him clear of the kill zone, but the medic was unable to save him. This hit the medic really hard. The boys know this because at night, they hear her crying in her sleep.

11th January 2012: In the Military, You Check In Twice

We left Dustystan in the dark of night. In the military, you check in twice. On the first occasion, you get rid of your hold luggage and acquire your boarding pass. That done, you return to your transit accommodation with your daysack which should contain overnight gear in the event that your flight is delayed.

When you check in on the second occasion, your daysack joins the rest of your luggage in the hold. Except it is not a hold but a large pallet upon which sits all the bags contained in a net. You then experience a further wait that is measured in hours before you join the aircraft attired in your body armour and helmet.

This is necessary as the Taliban likes to shoot at aircraft, which I am reliably informed are not armoured; hence we have to be. Flying inside a large cargo plane such as a C-17 is a unique experience. There is no air hostess service unless you fancy your chances with a burly loadmaster. I'll leave out describing the ablutions, which are a step up from a C-130 but not by much. We landed in the Middle East for another wait measured in hours, after which we transferred to a charter aeroplane.

This was a far more comfortable mode of transport although there was no club class. By now, we had been effectively awake the entire night, but I did manage to doze off on route to Cyprus. On arrival, we were taken off the aircraft and bussed to more transit accommodation, where we showered and had our dirty linen taken away for laundering.

Then it was breakfast and some decompression activities. The boys and girls were offered ten-pin bowling, horse riding, swimming, a visit to the gym or clay pigeon shooting. The go-karting, however, was cancelled. It had rained heavily and, therefore, for reasons of safety, was withdrawn as an activity. There may have been a few wry smiles. The Army is happy for you to go for a walk down a lane looking for IEDs, but heaven forbid that you should drive a go-kart after it's been raining.

There were a number of takers for the clay pigeon shooting. I'd have thought we'd all had quite enough of shooting; thank you very much but obviously not. Once the activities were concluded, we were bussed to a camp, which hosts the decompression.

I have to say, the military has pushed the boat out, and I'm typing this missive on one of the computers made available to the boys and girls. The accommodation is clean, and it has the added bonus of there being no chance of you getting lonely. They are selling beer tokens shortly. You source your ale using tokens. In this way, consumption is managed. You cannot access the ale until after we have had our counselling lectures, which start shortly. There is an excellent set-up here, and the folks who run it genuinely care for the troops.

That said, the only counselling I need is four pints of real ale at the Green Man. Sadly my levity on the matter does not do the subject justice. I only wish that were so. Yesterday on a British Forces Broadcasting Service news bulletin, we were told that 7200 of us would suffer from post-traumatic stress disorder as a consequence of Iraq and Afghanistan. Multiply that by the family members affected, and that's a bucket load of unhappiness.

12th January 2012: The Word Love is Not Out of Context

I have just been briefed that we shall be up at "oh my gosh, it's early". The Warrant Officer giving the brief was very kind in that he advised us not to set our alarm clocks because if the plane was delayed, he'd allow us to sleep on in oblivion.

The psychiatric nurse has also given his briefing, and we have been told what to be aware of on our return. The Padre followed and held nothing back. The poor chap covered the difficult subject of intimacy between a soldier and his wife after a period of prolonged absence. I'm now all clued up on that front but will, I'm sure, make a Horlicks of it.

The beer has been issued in accordance with the tokens with the warning that stripping naked would not be tolerated. It is a custom within the Royal Marines that on the command "naked bar" the lads all simultaneously strip off.

Apparently, at a recent combined services entertainment event, this caused a bit of a to-do when dozens of naked commandos stormed the stage when the band were doing their turn. Fortunately, we were light on commandos this evening, which allowed the two comedians and subsequent duet to entertain the throng without mishap.

The comics were excellent and have given me plenty of material to amuse the bell tower on my return. The duet was equally superb and obviously liked the feedback from the audience. As I watched the soldiers enjoying the event and revelling in each other's company, I was struck by a profound observation.

They are more than just fond of one another; rather, they cherish each other. In fact, the word love is not out of context here, which must make the loss in the battle of one of their number extraordinarily painful.

13th January 2012: And the Doctor's Regimental Number is What, Sir?

"Right, sir, if you'd just like to strip down and clean your weapons for inspection prior to the armoury, then that would be great."

I'd arrived back in Nottingham for my out-processing. I explained that I'd brought a colleague's weapon with me to save him the trouble of extending his tour by a further ten hours. This didn't seem to impress the Colour Sergeant, who viewed weapon husbandry as very much a personal responsibility. My explanation that it belonged to the doctor was met with a knowing glance and the instruction that it would also need to be cleaned.

I added that it was a waste of time for the two of us to come all this way. After all, the doctor had spent his tour saving the lives of our soldiers, so it was the least I could do. As I started stripping down my assault rifle, I was joined by two lads who worked on the doctor's pistol. They'd taken the point. He being a medic meant I was not surprised that on final reconciliation of his weapon and ancillaries, he was deficient of one holster. The return of this errant item I negotiated with his wife over the phone to the satisfaction of the SQMS. He had, after all, offered to settle matters through the raising of a bill.

Once I'd handed in my "gats", I went to the QM's store to return my body armour. Two sets for the use of.

"They'll need to be stripped down too, sir, if you'd be so kind. And the doctor's regimental number is what, sir?"

I responded by consulting my notebook in which I'd asked the doctor to put in his details. I'm sure I mentioned his regimental number but got two telephone numbers instead.

The Senior NCO gave me a look of resigned resignation before sending me off to the Regimental admin office, where I discovered that the Queen was about to short change me to the tune of £100 and that I was entitled to a refund on my Council Tax.

I was also given my Op HERRICK medal, which glittered in its box. My final visit was to the motor transport pool where a young lad issued me with a hire car for the onward journey.

"You'll need to fill it up prior to collection, sir, and do note the following scratches."

Lastly, I reported once again to the Colour Sergeant, who checked that all the signatures on my out-processing sheet were in order.

"Have a safe trip, sir."

I set off on the final leg of my journey as dark was beginning to settle. The warrant officer in Cyprus who'd advised us not to set our alarms in case the plane was delayed had proved prescient. It was, and we were left slumbering on.

Glowing Things to Say About Our Soldiers

On the flight home, I had fallen into conversation with an RAF medic who was part of a Medical Emergency Response Team (MERT), which includes a doctor and some lads doing force protection. They operate out of a Chinook helicopter equipped with intensive care medical facilities.

When one of our troops is hurt, this flying ambulance goes to recover him or her. They will also recover injured Afghans. When approaching the given LZ, the lads may still be in contact and if necessary, Apache attack helicopters will

418

be used to stabilise the situation. This paramedic had nothing but glowing things to say about our soldiers who are doing a fantastic job in providing initial care for those injured.

A little too much detail perhaps for one who'd had an airline meal but nevertheless reassuring. He raved about the "combat codpiece" which is doing so much to protect our wedding tackle. He tailed off though, when he mentioned the children.

"You see, the point at which the leg is severed from the body is head height to the young children. When they activate an IED, they are sort of obliterated, and there isn't much I can do."

He then went on to explain what he does do. I will, however, spare you the details.

For Those Who I Have Left Behind

As I drove into my home village, words fail to describe the sense of relief. To my reader in the Green Man, thank you for your support.

You'll understand if I declare that I'm not minded to write a sequence to these postings, so I hope you enjoyed them. Do say hello when you see me cutting about completing a six-month backlog of chores. If you find yourself in Church, put a little word in for our soldiers still out there and for those who I have left behind.

God Save the Queen.

Epilogue

Lieutenant Colonel Lyndon Robinson was, after all, never selected for redundancy. Quite the contrary, in fact. Once he'd concluded his 34-year engagement in 2018, he was asked to remain in post as a Garrison Commanding Officer for a further two years. On handing over to his successor, he was again asked to extend this time for a further six months. The reason was to allow him to undertake an assignment aimed at supporting the NHS as they struggled to fight the Covid-19 pandemic. In November 2020, he finally retired and now lives quietly in the countryside, tending his vegetable patch and giving his time voluntarily in support of the community, cadets and church.

This idyllic pastoral existence is in direct contrast to that being experienced by a highly regarded colleague with whom he served in Afghanistan. For that officer, the body came home, but the mind didn't.

June 2021

Lightning Source UK Ltd.
Milton Keynes UK
UKHW021835041021
391658UK00008B/57